A Commentary on
HEBREWS

UNLOCKING THE NEW TESTAMENT

A *Commentary on*
HEBREWS

David Pawson

Anchor Recordings

First published in Great Britain in 2014 by
Anchor Recordings Ltd
72 The Street
Kennington, Ashford TN24 9HS

**For more of David Pawson's teaching,
including MP3s, DVDs and CDs, go to
www.davidpawson.com
For further information,
email info@davidpawsonministry.com**

ISBN 978-1-909886-33-9

Printed by Lightning Source

Contents

This book is based on a series of talks. Originating as it does from the spoken word, its style will be found by many readers to be somewhat different from my usual written style. It is hoped that this will not detract from the substance of the biblical teaching found here.

As always, I ask the reader to compare everything I say or write with what is written in the Bible and, if at any point a conflict is found, always to rely upon the clear teaching of scripture.

David Pawson

A. NEGATIVE CONTRAST (1–10)
"DON'T GO BACK"

1. Son to servants (1–6)
Better than:
prophets; angels; apostles (Moses and Joshua);
priests (Aaron and sons)

2. Substance to shadows (7–10)
Better than:
priesthood (Melchizedek);
covenant (new);
sacrifices (once-for-all)

B. POSITIVE CONTINUITY (11–13)
"DO GO ON"

1. Faith in God
Abel, Enoch, Noah, Abraham, Isaac, Jacob,
Moses, Joseph, Joshua, Rahab, Gideon,
Barak, Samson Jephthah, David,
Samuel and the prophets

2. Focus on Jesus
Pioneer and perfecter of faith
Mediator of a new covenant
Sufferer outside the camp

INTRODUCTION

A. DIFFICULTY
1. Unknown background
   a. Author   b. Date   c. Destination
2. Unfamiliar ideas
   a. Hebrew – sacrifice   b. Greek – substance
B. QUESTION
1. Judaism – Old Testament
2. Christianity – New Testament
C. ANSWER
1. Continuity – Bible – salvation
2. Contrast – "better" – Son
D. PURPOSE
1. Negative – don't go back
2. Positive – do go on
E. VALUE
1. Exposes religion
2. Interprets scripture
3. Cures sacerdotalism
4. Stimulates growth
5. Uplifts Christ

The letter to the Hebrews is not the most popular New Testament book, although some passages are widely known, such as those in chapter 11 on the heroes of faith —Abraham, Moses and others, building up to that tremendous crescendo in the next chapter about running the race and looking to Jesus, the pioneer and the perfecter of our faith. Many know that chapter, and some know a few other texts.

Why is it that, on the whole, people do not like this book best? I would go as far as to say that you either love it as a whole or you tend to ignore it. It is because there is a very real difficulty: I think that it is the most difficult book in the New Testament (not excluding the book of Revelation). It is the most *theological* book — the one that, in a sense, most stretches your mind.

One of the difficulties is that the book has an unknown background. We don't know who wrote it, nor exactly when they wrote it, and we are not told who the first readers were, though many have tried to guess. So the difficulty is partly that we cannot get hold of the real life situation behind the letter. But we can go some way towards answering these questions.

First of all, who wrote it? In the Authorized Version it says: The Epistle of Paul to the Hebrews. But that, I am afraid, is an addition, and it is highly unlikely that Paul wrote this letter. It is quite different from his style. In fact, he wrote pretty rough and ready Greek, called Koine Greek, whereas Hebrews is written in beautiful, classical style by someone who obviously had a very good Greek education. There have been other suggestions. Some have suggested Barnabas, because this letter is most encouraging. It is described in the letter itself as a word of exhortation, and that means encouragement. Barnabas was a real man of encouragement and exhortation. Could it be him? It might be. Another suggestion is that Apollos wrote this —a man who was learned in the scriptures, who knew how to handle the Old Testament in a Christian way. So Apollos may have written this book. Another suggestion is that Luke wrote it. There are some similarities of style, and Luke was certainly able to handle the Greek language, but there is not a lot to be said for that one. Somebody else said that Priscilla wrote it, and because it might not be accepted as from a woman's hand she left her name off the letter. That is an intriguing and ingenious suggestion, but I don't think it carries any more weight.

The suggestion I like best, and which has a lot to commend it, is that it was written by Silas, who was associated with both Peter and Paul. Silas knew Jerusalem well, had a Greek education and was a Jew steeped in the Jewish scriptures. Everything about Silas fits this letter and I am impressed with that suggestion. But we don't really know. A scholar who said about sixteen hundred years ago that "God only knows who wrote this letter" was stating precisely the truth.

Can we work out the date? Can we put it in its context historically? I think we can go a little way towards doing so. It is like a detective story. It is quite obvious from the way Hebrews is written that the temple was still standing in Jerusalem. It was destroyed in AD 70, so we can set that as a latest possible date. We can set an early date because it is sent to people who have been Christians many years and by now ought to have grown up and matured – and not be on milk any more, but on meat. So it is the second generation of Christians. Therefore we can say that the earliest date is AD 50. Can we narrow it still further? I think we can. I think we can boil it down to about the mid-sixties because it says in this letter that the Christians have suffered loss of property but have not yet suffered unto blood. That means Christians had begun to suffer but had not yet been martyred. Can we date that? Yes, we can – the earliest martyrdoms began in the mid-sixties when Nero began to blame the great fire of Rome on the Christians. Since about AD 45 in Rome they had begun to experience loss of property. In Jerusalem they had been turned out of their homes and had to flee for their lives. So we have narrowed it down, and I think about the mid-sixties would be right.

Can we say anything about the people to whom it was written? This will help us to read it through their eyes. That it is written to the *Hebrews* is definite. It is written to Christians, so we can say it is written to Jews who have become Christians. Can we say anything more about them? Yes, we can say one very big thing: *they have come out of Judaism, but not fully; they have come into Christianity, but not fully, and this is the basic problem for which the letter is written.*

Even if we are not Jews we will get the message of the letter: leave your old life behind, including your religion, and go all the way with Christ; if you only go half way you will tend to drift away. So it was written to those who had not fully left Judaism and had not fully entered Christianity and who were still keeping a foot in both camps.

If ever you have been swimming when the water is cold, you will notice there are two kinds of swimmer. There are those who take a running leap and splash, and come up gasping and say, "It's wonderful, come on in!" Then there are those who climb down the steps, look utterly miserable and don't go any further. Those are the people who will hang around in the shallow end, and as soon as possible get out again and go and change back into their clothes. This is the basic problem here: it is a people who have not left their old life fully behind and have not yet matured fully into Christ. Therefore, having got in half way, they are a bit miserable and they are in danger of being discouraged and drifting away.

The writer is concerned about these Jewish Christians who *half* come over to Christ. He is going to try to show them that even the finest of their old religion needs to be left behind now. Christ is all they need. They must run the race looking to him, and they must not be discouraged because persecution is coming. It has already begun, they have lost their property, they have not yet resisted unto blood, and they may lose their lives shortly. It is vital that when persecution is looming you don't have "half and half" Christians with one foot in their old life and one foot in the new. You have to run the race looking to Jesus only. Surrounded as we are with such a cloud of witnesses, we have got to set our eyes and go all out if we are not going to be discouraged and drift away. Even though we are not Jews, the message will be just as relevant to us as it was to them.

Where were these Jewish Christians? Some have thought it was written to Jerusalem because that is where most of the Jewish Christians were. But I believe it was written to Rome, for there was a group within the church of Rome who were very strong Jewish Christians. There was a real Jewish colony there — something like 80,000 Jews — and some of them turned to Christ. If you study Paul's letter to the Romans, you realise that half the church is Gentile and half is Jewish. It is the Jewish half in the church of Rome that I believe this letter is addressed to. Because they are half and half, they are in danger of leaving the assembly, getting out from under their leadership there, and going back to their Jewish religion because it was safer.

In Rome an edict had been made meaning Judaism was a legally registered religion. But Christianity was illegal, like the underground church in some countries today. So these Jewish Christians knew that if they just stepped back on to the Jewish side of their life, they could be safe from persecution. But the author of Hebrews is saying: if you do that you will separate from the assembly, you will lose the leaders in Christ that you have. More seriously, the price for returning to the synagogue was a public denial that Jesus was the Jewish Messiah, tantamount to joining those Jews who crucified him for this claim. Drop your Judaism and, whatever it costs, go all the way with Christ. Get right into the Christian side of your life, and then you are ready for persecution.

Now I believe that persecution may well be on its way in this country and may hit us within our lifetime. Therefore this letter has a message to us to get right into the assembly and go all the way with Jesus, looking unto him, the pioneer and perfecter of our faith, and then we will not drift and not be discouraged. Why do I think it must have been Rome? It not only fits the situation, but at the end of the letter the author says, "Those who come from Italy send their greetings to you." I think that is a pretty clear indication that it was written to the church in Rome.

Having looked at the basic background as far as the difficulties of the letter goes, not only is the unknown background a difficulty, but secondly, the unfamiliar ideas in this book are a difficulty. We are dealing with ideas with which we are not familiar in the twenty-first century. Take first a Hebrew idea which runs right through the letter, just as a scarlet thread ran through every rope used in the Royal Navy — running right through this letter is a scarlet thread called "sacrifice".

That was a Hebrew idea and it was also a pagan idea. Visiting Brazil many years ago, I came out one morning from the Wycliffe Bible Translation Headquarters in Brasilia, and there, outside the gate in the dusty road, was a broken bowl with the remains of cockerels and even dogs. I knew that a sacrifice had been offered during the night by some black magic practitioners, right outside the gate of that Christian establishment. There was a sense of evil there— 60% of the population were engaged in spiritism. I looked at the remains of birds and animals, and the whole thing was repulsive to me because I have never been used to sacrifice in religion. Neither have you, I expect. If you see a video, brought back by some missionary, of an animal having its throat cut and the blood going everywhere, I find that church people in this country usually close their eyes or turn away at that point. We are not used to it.

If we had blood all over the table at the front of our church building, and dead animals lying around the front, like an abattoir, you would be worried. We just don't like blood, we don't like killing. We eat meat for Sunday lunch, but we try to forget where it came from. We don't connect it up; it came in a plastic container from the supermarket, it didn't come from an abattoir.

So we have this nice, respectable attitude now and we keep it all hidden, but in those days sacrifice was a vital part of religion, and it is only because Christ died that we don't have it now. All this emphasis on blood and offering and sacrifice, and goats and bulls being slaughtered – this is a strange world for us to live in. But don't believe that you will understand the cross of Christ unless you get back into this idea and get the feel of the blood that needs to be spilled in order that a sinner might come to God.

There is another idea that to us is a bit unfamiliar and strange, from the Greek world, namely the Greek idea of "substance" which comes into this letter again and again. The idea of the Greeks about substance is this. We would say a wooden pulpit is a real lump of substance. The Greeks would look at it and say: no, this pulpit is only a shadow; the substance of the pulpit is somewhere else. This is only a copy of the real thing, which is in some spiritual world, some heavenly place. To us Westerners, the real world is this world and the shadowy, unreal world is the other world. That is so burnt into our thinking that however much we talk about heaven it always seems a little bit unreal; the local High Street seems more real to us. The Greeks, and notably the philosopher Plato, thought the other way around. The Greeks said that the trees and streets are unreal — shadows.

They are only poor copies of the real thing, which exists in the spiritual world. That idea is taken up by the author to the Hebrews. He uses it to say that all the sacrifices on earth were just copies of the real one; that even the tabernacle itself and the temple were just copies of the Holy of Holies in heaven, which is the real one. So what we deal with in this world are shadows, types, copies, imitations, and the real thing is in heaven. In Jesus, however, the real in heaven came to earth and the real sacrifice took place. We have the real high priest, the real sacrifice — and the real altar is not here now on earth, but is in heaven. It is through Jesus our high priest that we come to God.

That is a world of ideas that is strange to us. We almost have to pinch ourselves and then say: but that is not real, that is the shadow. The real thing is somewhere else. In fact the real, eternal body that I am going to have is not this one; this is only a copy of it. This won't last for long, one day I will get rid of this body. I will be finished with it; I will get the real thing one day.

We come, secondly, to the main question that Hebrews asks and answers. The basic question concerns the relationship between Judaism and Christianity, the Old Testament and the New Testament. That is a very important question to get answered. Otherwise, you can get a lot of things wrong. What is the relationship between the temple and the church? What is the relationship between the Jews and Jesus? This was bound to arise for a number of reasons. First, many of the unbelievers were Jewish, as was Jesus and as were the twelve apostles. Some early Christians were converted Jewish priests. What were they to do about their priesthood?

Another reason is that after Pentecost the early Christians went on using the temple for prayers every day. It was obviously the only building that was big enough to contain the Christian church in Jerusalem, which numbered five thousand after a few months. But going to the temple was bound to raise the question: what about all these sacrifices still going on in there? Do we Christians take any part in that? A further reason is that at that period the only Bible that the church had was the Old Testament; the New Testament was not written for some decades after Jesus died and rose again.

Yet another reason was that when all the Gentile believers came into the church they were bound to say, "Do we have to become Jewish in order to become Christian?" This was one of the deepest issues that almost divided the early church into two denominations. If you study the book of Acts, within Jerusalem itself the Jewish believers and the Gentile believers pulled apart until things got more and more serious. Paul had to resist Peter on this question and he had to write the Epistle to the Galatians, and he had to go to Jerusalem, and they held two councils on this matter before they settled it. Praise God, the Holy Spirit kept them from dividing.

There were those who wanted to keep certain Jewish laws. The Sabbath is a Jewish matter, but as soon as we raise the question about Sabbath observance we get all shades of viewpoint, including those who say the Christian is subject to the fourth commandment ("Remember the Sabbath day to keep it holy") and others who say the Christian has nothing to do with that. Hebrews chapter 4 deals with the matter of Sabbath observance.

The first Christian to die for the faith was stoned to death because he said Christians were not bound by Jewish custom. His name was Stephen. The teaching of Stephen is very close to this letter to the Hebrews. Some even thought he may have written it, but it was written after he died. What is the answer, then, to this difficult question: how do the Old Testament and New Testament relate? The answer is two-fold: There is both *continuity* and *contrast*. You have to have both. The continuity lies in the fact that God gave the Old and God gave the New, and it is the same God speaking. The contrast lies in the fact that God was giving types and shadows and copies in the Old, and that the real substance came in the New. As Hebrews begins: in the Old Testament, God gave his word in bits and pieces. But in the New Testament, he put it all together.

When you have the sacrifice of Christ on the cross, then the sacrifice of bulls and goats falls away. Christianity grew out of a Judaistic background and the Bible came to us written by Jews. Jesus, God the Son, was and is a Jew. Yet Christians do not become Jewish in order to know this Jewish God.

The letter to the Hebrews underlines the contrast with just two key words, which appear all the way through. If you don't mind underlining in your Bible (I hope you don't), then mark these two words whenever we get to them: *better*, and *Son*.

The first key word, *better* or, in some translations, *superior* occurs thirteen times. We have someone who is "better" than the angels, "better" than Moses, "better" than Joshua, "better" than Aaron. We have a better sacrifice than bulls and goats. We have a better covenant than the Old Covenant—better, better, better!

Of course, if you read between the lines, the author is really saying "best". But the contrast is there – "better". The Christian way is better than the Jewish way, for Christ is so much better than all the people who were sent to help the Jews.

But *why* is Jesus better? The answer is very simple. Here is the second key word: because he is the *Son*. The angels — are they not ministering servants? Moses — was he not a servant? Joshua — was he not a servant? The priests — were they not servants? The high priest — was he not a servant? But we have the Son, and to have the Son of God is so much better than having the servants of God.

The Old Testament tells of many servants of God, tremendous heroes of faith. But when you have looked at them all and learned everything you can from them all, turn your eyes away from this cloud of witnesses and look to Jesus, the Son.

So, the letter to the Hebrews is saying: you can leave your Judaism behind, leave your heroes of faith behind, leave these men behind, and turn to Jesus, go all the way with Jesus, and run the race right to the end. Then you won't drift because you have got someone far better. You have an anchor within the veil to your soul. You have someone to hang on to. All those other servants passed from the scene, they came and they went. But Jesus abides, a priest forever—he stays with you.

There is a practical purpose in this letter. It is not academic theology, but sandwiched into a fairly theological argument, and every now and again there are practical exhortations as to how you put this into practice. For example, having talked about Jesus being, as the Son, superior to all the angels, how is that applied practically? The author writes: "How shall we escape if we neglect so great a salvation?" Fully down to earth, you see. Suddenly it is put into your life. Christ is so much better than the angels; you may never have heard about angels, but you have heard about Christ. And therefore, if that is so much better, how then shall we escape if we neglect what is even better than the Jews had? The better the religion, the more serious it is to ignore it. Since we have the best salvation of all, how shall we escape if we neglect it? Hearing about Christ puts a greater responsibility on us than on the Jews. Now this epistle is called a word of *exhortation*, and therefore it is divided in its practical side between the negative exhortations which are warning us, and the positive exhortations which are wooing us to Christ. Warning us of drifting; wooing us closer to him.

There is a warning of neglect, a warning against unbelief, a warning against disobedience, a warning against immaturity, a warning against rejection, and a warning against refusal.

One of the most serious passages, and one of the most difficult, is in Hebrews chapter 6, which warns that it is possible to have gone through the motions of becoming a Christian, to have tasted of the powers of the age to come, and then to fall away. It says most solemnly if that happens to you, there is no hope of coming back again. That is something more serious than just backsliding, it is apostasy. It says you can get far enough into the Christian faith to have tasted of the powers of the age to come, but if you turn back then you crucify the Lord afresh and there is no-one left to save you and no hope of repentance. It is a solemn practical warning.

On the positive side, however, the wooing always begins with two little words: *Let us*.... Here are some of the positive exhortations: "Let us fear..."; "Let us give diligence to enter..."; "Let us hold fast our confession..."; "Let us draw near to the throne of grace..."; "Let us press on to perfection..."; "Let us hold fast the confession of our faith"; "Let us consider one another..."; "Let us lay aside every weight..."; "Let us run the race..."; "Let us have grace..."; "Let us go forth unto him..."; "Let us offer up sacrifice of praise...." — "Let us ... let us".

All the way through Hebrews we find such pleas. I hope that, as we go through this letter, your heart will respond and say: yes, let's do this.

This is therefore at once the most stern and the most tender book in the New Testament. It has the harshest warnings and the most tender appeals.

Finally, we consider the *value* of this book. Five things show us what Hebrews can do for people, demonstrating that this book is not irrelevant (though we are not Jewish Christians), nor is it out of date.

First: this book *exposes religion*. Religion is a copy, and Judaism is the best copy there was, but Hebrews exposes all religion as copy – unreal. It is saying: when you come to Christ you leave your religion behind. That is a lesson that many don't learn, but it is part of that which falls away. Even though your religion may be a well-nigh perfect copy, as Judaism was, then you still leave it behind when you have got the real thing. Too often, religion creeps back in to our Christianity and we become religious again. Religion is the enemy of Christianity.

Have you noticed that unbelievers get religious? Unbelievers, who only go to church three times a year, when they do go, want something very religious. They dress up for the occasion and they go through all the rites and ceremonies, and they like that kind of ritualistic religion. Why? Because they haven't got the real thing, so they like the copies, and of course you need the copies when you haven't got the real thing. When you are not a believer, when you don't have faith, you have got to have the visible. You have got to have something to look at, whereas faith is the substance of things hoped for, the evidence of things *not* seen.

Therefore, those who come to a service by faith don't need a lot of vestments, you don't need the sacrifice, you don't need the copies; you have got faith in the real God. That is why unbelievers can come to a service and say; "Well, it wasn't religious enough for me." Of course it wasn't, we only want the reality; we have left religion behind. Let us draw near to God; let us draw near to Christ.

Secondly, *this book interprets scripture for us*. If you have sat down to read the Bible right through, you may have got a bit stuck in Leviticus. But that very book comes alive and is full of meaning for you after reading Hebrews. The sacrifices begin to have meaning because you are reading about them as copies of the real thing and Hebrews helps you to understand the real thing, the sacrifice of Christ. So, you look at the burnt offering, the meal offering, the peace offering, the sin offering, the guilt offering, and suddenly you see all five aspects of the cross. The cross is the real thing that includes them all. So it interprets scripture for us and it gives us great help with the part of scripture we find most difficult – the Old Testament.

Thirdly, *it cures sacerdotalism*. That is an ecclesiastical word which in simple terms means, "Going High Church". High Churchianity is simply a reversion to the unreal copies. It is going back to the Old Testament, to altars and priests and incense and all the rest. In Christ we don't need that any more.

Fourthly, the letter to the Hebrews *stimulates spiritual growth*. Right there at the end of Hebrews chapter 5 it is saying: don't go on being babies, don't want a bottle of milk every time you come to church; you should be ready for meat. The whole of the letter to the Hebrews is an appeal to Christians to grow up and become strong, so it stimulates growth, and particularly, if I may say so, this is for second-generation Christians. Perhaps your parents, grandparents or great-grandparents were Christians. But the peril of being a second generation Christian is that you may slowly drift away from your parents' faith, that you never get as far into it as they got. You may be religious, and have the form but not the power of godliness, so that by the third generation the parents' faith can get lost.

Hebrews is written for second generation Christians — for those who can remember great Christian leaders who have died and are no longer with us. It is saying: remember them and imitate their faith; get up to their standard, go as far as they went. Go all the way with Jesus. Don't rest on their faith, don't have a second-hand religion.

The final value of the letter to the Hebrews is that *it uplifts Christ*. Christ is prominent on every page. At every stage of the argument, your eyes are turned to Christ. Whether we are discussing Moses, Joshua, Aaron, Melchizedek, or all the heroes of faith, every time: your eyes are turned to Jesus. Fix your gaze on *him* and look to *him* for the rest of your life and the rest of your race.

This is why Hebrews has sometimes been called the "fifth Gospel". If Matthew, Mark, Luke and John tell us about his ministry on earth, then Hebrews tells us about his ministry in heaven. Therefore, Hebrews is the only book in the New Testament to concentrate on one particular aspect of Christ: the Gospels talk about him as Saviour and King, the other epistles talk about him as Lord, but *in this letter we see him as our priest.*

We should not talk about our church leaders as priests. We are all priests in a sense — all believers in Jesus have access to God. But we have one high priest, and we must not forget that Christ is our priest in heaven and that we cannot approach God without a priest—no-one can—and that you need to confess your sins to Jesus Christ the priest. Let us not forget that, it is part of Christianity. *Hebrews uplifts the priesthood of Jesus Christ.*

I believe that is why the author did not include his name. He was known to his readers, he did not want to remain anonymous, but I think he wanted all his readers to turn their attention on to the Lord Jesus Christ and look to him. So as we go through Hebrews we are going to look at Jesus Christ and we are going to run toward him, and we are going to grow in grace and in the knowledge of our Lord.

1

BETTER THAN PROPHETS
Read 1:1–3

A. OLD WORDS – THE PROPHETS (1)
1. Many fragments
2. Many forms
B. NEW WORD – A SON (2–3)
1. Creation (totality)
    a. Heir of its consummation
    b. Agent of its creation
2. Creator (deity)
    a. Reflection of his brightness
    b. Stamp of his being
3. Creatures (humanity)
    a. Saviour with a cross (atonement)
    b. Lord with a crown (ascension)

The epistle to the Hebrews tells us, firstly, why Christianity is better than any other religion, including Judaism; secondly, how the Old Testament is related to the New Testament; thirdly, who Jesus is and what he did. These three things have a very practical object in the heart and in the will.

The first people to read this letter were those who had left their old religion and come into Christianity – but they had not quite left it and they had not quite got in. They were in a kind of no-man's land in between, and that is a miserable place to be. They were just at that point where the first honeymoon with Jesus was over and they had begun to realise what they had lost in Jesus and what they had left behind. Their heart was tugging back a little to the security of the religion in which they had been brought up. Most of us go through this stage, I think. Not usually at first—usually for the first two to three months the Lord protects us from too much attack until we are on our feet. But then comes the crisis and the tug between the old and the new, the flesh and the Spirit, the world we have left and the world we have entered. We begin to wonder — have we really given all that up? We feel insecure, and the letter to the Hebrews is written to tell us not to look back. Go on, run the race, look to Jesus! Don't drift because you have suddenly realised that you have left so much behind. You have in fact got something far better. What you have dropped is just a handful of mud. So the teaching about Jesus in this letter is really with a very practical objective: to send us on in the Lord, because being a Christian is like riding a bicycle—if you don't go on, you'll come off.

For the readers of this letter there was a pressing incentive to revert to their former way of life. They were Jews who had come to faith in their Messiah, Jesus. They had therefore transferred from the synagogue to the church. But Judaism was tolerated by the Romans (a "religio licita", legal) while Christianity was not (a "religio illicita", illegal). So they had exchanged safety for insecurity. Persecution had begun, from looting to imprisonment – but not yet martyrdom.

For the protection of their families, the temptation to return to the synagogue and become "secret" believers there must have been great. However the price for doing so was to make a public confession of their mistaken conversion, tantamount to declaring that Jesus was not the Messiah (the Christ), an act of apostasy from which there could be no recovery, according to this writer (6:4–6). It is his most serious warning.

Hebrews is unique. There is no name, no address and no greeting. It is as if the writer cannot wait to get into his subject. He has to get right into the main theme, and he does so within the first sentence. What a sentence! It is the finest classical Greek in the whole of the New Testament, magnificently constructed in beautiful language, so much so that translators have been unable to render it in one English sentence adequately. Its majesty and beauty matches its subject.

In the Bible the existence of God is nowhere argued for, it is always taken for granted. The problem is not why God exists but why anything else exists! Having said that, there is a particular thing said about God in this sentence which thrills me. It is in two words: "God spoke...." If he had not done so, we would be in awful trouble. Most people believe in some kind of god but they do not know him. Why not? Because God has not spoken to them, or if he has, they have not listened or they have not heard and they have been deaf to his call. But how do you get to know a person? You get to know them when they speak to you.

Any minister can find, as I did, that most church members know him better than he knows them. That is partly because of numbers. Each member knows him but he may have a few hundred to know. But he speaks to them more than they do to him because he preaches – and if I am speaking I am bound to be revealing myself, my strengths and weaknesses, faults and failures. A congregation gets to know me because I speak. Mind you, if I gave a very carefully prepared address and read every word then my hearers would not get to know me as well. How you get to know anyone is not just by looking at them or thinking about them but by letting them talk to you. If God did not speak then we would never get to know him intimately. ***But God wants to be known. He wants to speak to you, and he wants you to listen.***

What ties the Old and the New Testament together in continuity is that from the beginning to the end of the Bible God spoke. If we listen to what he said then we get to know him intimately. The relationship between the Testaments is both continuity and contrast: the *continuity* is that God spoke in both Testaments; the *contrast* is that God spoke through prophets in the past, and through his Son in the New. The same God spoke in both Testaments but in different ways. That is why the Old Testament can never be the same as the New Testament. The New Testament is better than the Old – not morally better, not spiritually better, but better because God spoke through his Son in the New Testament. We will see in what sense it is better and in what sense it isn't.

Hebrews draws seven contrasts between the Old and the New Testament, seven ways in which Christ is better than anybody who went before. The first contrast is between *Christ and the prophets*. The second will be between *Christ and the angels*. The third will be between *Christ and Moses*. The fourth will be between *Christ and Joshua*. The fifth will be between *Christ and Aaron* and so it will go on.

We begin with the first contrast which only takes three verses to state – angels takes a little longer and priests take much longer.

If you had lived in the Old Testament days you could have heard God speaking, but in a very different way to the way he speaks to you today. Let's then look at the old words of God: the Old Testament. The whole Bible is the Word of God or as I would prefer to say, the *words* of God because I think God inspired not just the Word generally but the words particularly. The Bible consists of the words of God but there are old words (Old Testament) and new words (New Testament) and we belong to the new era but the old words are all true.

We have to accept, first of all – and this is an offence to

modern man who is so universalist in his thinking – that the way God speaks is not to speak to everybody when he is giving a word of revelation, it is to speak to some and tell them to pass his word on to the others. So he doesn't simultaneously tell everybody the same thing. He tells maybe one person and says: now you pass it on. So out of all the nations of the world he spoke just to one. The Bible is not made up of revelations to the Chinese and the Indians and the Romans and the Greeks. It is made up of the revelation of God to Israel, just one little nation out of a whole lot. "God spoke to our fathers," says this writer to the Hebrews. He spoke to the Jews—that is an offence; it is one of the reasons why there is a feeling that the Jews are different, and there is a kind of jealousy deep down in the rest of the human race that one nation should be chosen to be the channel of God's revelation.

"But what advantage has the Jew?" says Paul. Everything in every way, "To him were delivered the oracles of God...." We have to accept the fact that God chooses to speak to all the nations through one nation. Within that one nation he did not speak to all the Jews but to a handful of men and women, and they spoke to the nation. This method ensures that we share the good things he gives us. If he had chosen to deal with every nation – if he had sent a messiah to America and a messiah to China – then we would isolate ourselves from each other. We have to come to those who have his word.

The old words were to the "fathers" in the past, through the prophets, who were great men of God. The more I read about the prophets the more stirred I am. I think of Isaiah. Do you know how he met his death? They put him in a hollow tree trunk and sawed him through—Hebrews 11 describes that, "Some were sawed asunder." I think of Jeremiah and how he was thrown into a pit and up to his waist in slimy mud, and left there because he preached the Word of God.

Prophet after prophet was stoned, killed, slain before the altar. These were men who sometimes stood alone even against the popular preachers of their day, but they were men who were given a word from God.

The Old Testament is simply not a collection of writings of history. It is a collection of the period of history and writings, from the first prophet to the last – beginning with the books of Moses and ending with the book of Malachi. There are other books of ancient history, which are interesting. But they are not in the Bible and they should not be because they are not the Word of God.

There is one phrase which occurs 3,808 times and ties every part of the Old Testament together: "Thus says the Lord" or, in the Hebrew, "Thus says *Yahweh* [I am]...." If God spoke through all those prophets over a period of 1,500 years or more, then surely that's enough? But no, it's not, because the very channel he used, human beings, inspired as they were, nevertheless had limitations. The word of the Old Testament has limitations. Let's look at what they are.

Let me say a little word about inspiration. I don't believe that God treated men as typewriters – robots – and just typed out on them his message, because the very personality of the prophets comes through their message. But what I do believe is that God so inspired the prophets that what they said – *including* their own personality coming through – was what he wanted said, exactly. The glory of inspiration to me is that God can use a person without obliterating their character, without removing their personal insights, but using that person in such a way that what they say is the perfect Word of God and utterly to be trusted. This is why in the New Testament you can pick out the stamp of Paul on his writings, and yet, as he says in those writings: what I say is not from me it's from the Lord and you have accepted it as such.

You can tell when Peter is writing a letter. He has his own style and John has his own style. Yet even though there is a personal style, the Lord so used these men that what they produced was his infallible Word and exactly what he wanted done. So God in his wonderful wisdom can use human personality to get his Word across. The limitations therefore do not lie in the direction in which some scholars suggest. The limitations of the Old Testament were not that some of the things they wrote were in error and needed to be corrected, and were primitive ideas. What were the limitations? They were two-fold: that the Word of God came in many fragments and in many forms. That is the literal translation of the Greek: "... many fragments and in many forms" — in bits and pieces, in a variety of media.

Let us look at those two statements. "Many fragments" — it is like a box that you open and there is a jigsaw with lots of little pieces. Therefore each piece is limited and you can only get a certain amount of message from that piece, but when another piece is added you get a little more of the message and a little more. So the revelation in the Old Testament is progressive — but that does not mean that it is evolutionary. I am stressing this because views on inspiration went haywire in the twentieth century.

The idea of progressive revelation to some means that from primitive misunderstandings you move to cultured understandings, and that therefore you leave behind primitive ideas of what God was saying — but I do not believe that. You don't leave anything behind when you add one piece of a jigsaw to the next. You don't cancel out the first piece. You may see it in a different light, and what you thought was a bit of this proves, when you add another piece, to be a bit of that, and the picture builds up. None of it needs cancelling as you find more bits in a jigsaw. But the full picture never came in the Old Testament. Bits of it came.

If Amos saw the justice of the Lord and Hosea saw the mercy of the Lord and Isaiah saw the holiness of the Lord and other prophets saw this bit and that bit, they were filling out the picture but they never got the whole of it. When it comes to the life of Jesus, you can find every major event in the life of Jesus in the Old Testament, but you have to search the Old Testament for it, and there is a bit here and a bit there: his birth here and his ministry there and his death and betrayal there and his resurrection there and his ascension there—you have to look all over the place in the law of Moses, in the prophets, in the Psalms. It was in many fragments. So it is not so easy to see the whole picture.

One of the dangers with the Old Testament is that you pick and choose bits and pieces, taking the bits you prefer and dropping the rest. So many people love some of the Psalms, especially the comforting ones (such as "The Lord is my Shepherd, I shall not want") but they don't like others. Even in one Psalm they pick bits and pieces. You probably know the Psalm: "If I ascend into heaven you are there and if I make my bed in Sheol you are there." It is a lovely Psalm but at the end it talks about hating one's enemies and the enemies of God with perfect hatred, and that bit we are not so sure of. I believe we should take all the pieces. When we turn to the New Testament, we have got the lid of the box with a picture on it. We have the whole picture in Jesus Christ.

So many *fragments*—that's a limitation on the Old Testament. Secondly, many *forms*. When you pick up your Old Testament you find that the Word of God comes in prose, poetry, proverbs, predictions, history, parable, laws, love songs, prayers, praises, visions, voices. The variety of media that God used! It makes for a very interesting book. Sometimes he spoke in thunder and sometimes in a gentle stillness. The many forms God used blend together beautifully.

If you consider that forty different authors wrote the Bible over a period of 1,400 years in at least three different languages, and consider that the whole thing hangs together and it had no editor except the Holy Spirit, it is a miracle in words. But it is a limitation that it is in many forms. What God wanted finally to do was to put all the truth in one form and that form was to be the form of a man and the form of a servant. That form contained the whole truth. In him was to dwell all the fullness of the godhead bodily.

So the poor people in the Old Testament had to listen to a little bit from this prophet and a little bit from that, and even the prophets themselves searched their own prophecies to try to see the whole picture and couldn't. Whereas they had to cope with many different forms of revelation, we have only one form and no fragments. We have the whole truth, so our Lord Jesus says, "I am the truth" — the whole lot, everything you need to know for your salvation is in Jesus. He is the truth.

Jesus is *logos* and that is a word we use of many areas of study (as in theology, zoology, biology, psychology, sociology and so on). The word "logos" and the suffix "-logy" are the same. Every branch of study is studying part of what Christ has created, because he upholds the universe. He created it and it is all going to him. Jesus Christ is the whole truth; everything that God knows is in Christ. Everything that God says is in Christ. So spare a thought for those who only have the Old Testament and those who can only see the bits and pieces. Pray for God's ancient people who don't have the New Testament — they cannot see the picture.

We have thought about the old words of God in the prophets. Now let us turn to the new word, "In these last days" — that was a technical term. It doesn't just mean that the writer was saying "in recent days". He is saying this: we have now entered the last period of human history, therefore God has spoken his final word. Over many centuries he spoke through the prophets, but now in just thirty-three years he said his last word. This is the Word of God now. That is why we don't go on adding to the Bible. That is why we don't say: we will have a loose-leaf Bible and add every new thing that is revealed about God. If you study mathematics, science or anything else and they gave you a 2,000-year old textbook and said, "That's the last word on the subject," you would laugh – but not in church, not with the truth, not with God. God has spoken his last word, and the witnesses to that last word were the apostles, and *we have the apostolic writings in the New Testament—that is his last word*. The firsthand witness to his final word ends the Bible. On the last page of it there is a curse on those who either take anything away from it or add anything to it. It is finished – final word, final period of history, God is not going to speak again in revelation. He may speak to us personally in application and guidance but not in revelation. Notice it says: "He spoke to our fathers through the prophets, but in these last days he has spoken to us". He is writing to people who never met Jesus personally in the flesh but he still includes them. He says "us" and that includes you and me. In these last days God has spoken to us through his Son. All believers are included, but by a Son — not through many people but by one person. Not through many fragments but through one complete whole. Not through many forms but through one person and what he said and did and does and is. That is the great contrast. How much better, therefore, this religion is than any other.

Of the major world religions, only one started after Jesus Christ, and that is Islam. It started nearly six hundred years after Jesus. Therefore Islam claims to be a better religion than Christianity. It claims to be a superior religion. That is why the Muslim countries are among the most difficult areas in the world for missionaries. They can labour for years and not get through. Islam says about Jesus that he is just one in the line of prophets. The letter to the Hebrews says that you can't get better than Christianity because God has spoken to us in his Son – not a prophet, but a Son – and to put Jesus among the prophets is to go backwards even if you do it six hundred years after he came.

We have only covered the first verse so far, and in the rest of these verses we have a three-dimensional view of Jesus the Son. Things are said about Jesus in vv. 2–3 that have never been said about any other man who has ever lived. They were never said about Mohammad, Buddha or Confucius, and they could not be because they were not true of those people. The things that are said here are either the biggest pack of lies that have ever been uttered about a man or they are the absolute truth.

I know that Hitler discovered that the bigger the lie you tell, the more that people will believe it, and that is true but only for a time. They pretty soon discover that it is a lie and then they disbelieve it. But the truths here! Nobody has ever proved them false. We are studying the sober truth. Remember that they are said of a man who walked this earth, who was born of a human mother, who walked the dusty roads, who talked, who lived thirty-three years right here. The three dimensions are these: his relationship to creation, his relationship to the Creator, and his relationship to the creatures who moved through his creation. I want to put it in another way: his relationship to the totality of things, his relationship to the deity, and his relationship to humanity. Look what is said about them.

Jesus must be more than a great man. A great man's significance is limited to the period from his birth to his death, but here, describing Jesus, Hebrews goes as far back as the human mind can conceive and as far forward as the human mind can conceive.

The furthest we can go back in thought is to the beginning of our universe; you cannot go further than that without getting in such a whirl in your mind that you are utterly confused. You can accept that there was a time before the universe but you cannot imagine what it was like, can you? The end of our universe is as far forward as you can think with ordinary human imagination.

So the letter to the Hebrews in describing our Lord's relationship to the creation, to the totality of created things, goes to these two extremes. A man who lived for thirty-three years in history and already our view is being stretched to both extremes. Funnily enough, Hebrews starts with the end extreme before the beginning. He goes to the end and says this, "God has made a will and named Jesus as the legatee of the entire universe, he is the heir of all things."

Now there is much speculation as to who is going to control the world ultimately. Who is going to get it all? The answer is very simple—Jesus. This world has many trust deeds for property, musty offices full of rolled up bits of paper with red ribbon around them. Arguments go on every day in the courts as to which bit belongs to who, but I tell you that one day the whole lot will belong to Jesus. This is an astonishing statement when you consider the poverty that he knew while he was on earth. We can almost say he only owned what he stood up in, and even that was taken from him at the end. Yet this man is to inherit all things – the whole lot. At the end of time everything will be his. That is either an utter lie or it is sober truth. The heir of all things appointed by God to inherit the entire estate. That is the first thing — to unite all things in him.

Now let us go right back to the beginning. He is not only the heir of all creation at the end; he was the agent of all creation at the beginning. Long before he was a carpenter making chairs and tables, he made the trees from which those chairs and tables were made. Long before he climbed the hills of Galilee, he made those hills. Long before he sailed the sea in a boat, he made that sea. He made the oceans as well. Long before he walked this earth, he hung it in space.

What about in between? He not only made all things in the beginning and will inherit them all at the end, but at this very moment he upholds all things. The sun rose this morning, or, as we know, the earth turned this morning, because Jesus holds it in his hand. He upholds planet earth.

The thing that struck me most forcibly about the trip to the moon and the photographs they brought back was to see earth hanging in nothing. Did that hit you? Earth seems so solid, and you think you have something underneath you now, but in fact we have got nothing underneath us, it is just there in space. Everything in our universe is moving. If I snap my fingers, you travelled nineteen miles in the same time. How are you feeling? Again, if you just believe what your senses tell you, you won't believe that. But you do believe it, don't you? Are you prepared to take the word of scientists that our earth is spinning through space? You have moved around a quarter of a mile in the past second. So we moved nineteen miles one way and a quarter of a mile another way in a second. You accept it by faith. People who say "I only believe what my senses tell me" don't really. They believe a whole lot of things. They believe what they want to believe, they take the scientists' word for it. This whole universe is on the move and these bodies are all moving through space according to a planned orbit. Who does it? This same Jesus who created it in the beginning, who will get it all in the end, upholds all things. The earth doesn't slip, because he holds it. No scientist can prove that statement and no scientist can disprove it. It is a matter of faith that we believe that the things that are seen were made out of things not seen, and out of nothing.

It is faith that believes Jesus holds this earth where it is and that he holds the oceans to their appointed limits where they are. We would only need the ice in the world to melt and the oceans would rise catastrophically. He upholds, he sustains, he orders all things. That is the first dimension of this view of Jesus in Hebrews. Do you accept that? Are you prepared to believe it? That is Jesus' relationship to the creation.

Now we think about Jesus' relationship to the Father. I recall a bookshop window in London displaying booklets entitled *The Man who was God* – and I wondered why people weren't shattered by that title.

There are two things said here. First, that Jesus was the reflection of his brightness. Can I put it very simply: what the sunshine is to the sun, Jesus is to God—that's what this phrase means. Look at the sunshine streaming in through a window. It has taken eight minutes for it to travel at a hundred and eighty-six thousand miles a second from the sun. So when you see the sun rise, it actually rose eight minutes before you saw it. It comes streaming in and we feel it and we benefit from it. It has reached earth and yet basically it is sunlight. Now there is a difference between moonlight and sunlight. Moonlight is reflected, sun is direct radiance, sunlight. This word means not that Jesus reflects God perfectly but that he actually shines God and that he has reached earth. He is God's sunbeam on earth. He is on earth and God is shining in his life. If you look at Jesus, you will see God shining.

Now frankly, if God was shining in Jesus as fully as God shines normally, you would not be able to look at Jesus. Not even the strongest sunglasses would help you. You know, of course, that you can't look directly at the sun. It is too bright and would blind you. You can bear to look at sunlight, but there were two occasions when actually God's glory shone so brilliantly in Jesus himself that they could hardly bear to look. One was when Peter, James, and John went up the mountain and Jesus' clothes changed not by reflecting light but by having so much light within them that they became transparent—that is the description. He was transfigured and they saw his glory – glory as of the only-begotten Son of God the Father. He was shining and even that was toned down so that they could bear to look. They couldn't have stood the full thing.

A few months later another man saw the glory of Christ and it was turned up even further. His name was Saul of Tarsus. It was midday and the sun was shining brightly but suddenly there was around him such a light that it was brighter than the midday sun. If you can imagine looking into something that is brighter than the midday sun, no wonder he was blinded. For three days he was in total darkness. His retina must have been really damaged, as we know he was healed three days later and given his sight back.

It was Paul's retina that would feel that bright light. He saw the glory of Jesus and said, "Who are you?" A voice said, "I am Jesus." He was the person that people used to look at in the street, of whom they could say, "Isn't that a carpenter?" Now it was with glory. Even that wasn't as bright as Jesus really is. When you get your resurrection body your eyes will be enough to cope with it and you will be able to look. But if you saw the glory of God straight, clear today, you couldn't take it. Jesus was God shining as much as people could bear, and in his shining face the radiance of God's glory shone.

The second thing is that he was the very stamp of God's being. This is an image taken from coins. If you pull a coin out of your pocket and look at the image of the sovereign on it, that's the stamp of the sovereign. My father was once taken on a surprise visit to a little studio where a lady was working, delicately shaping something with a large, round cast. She was the person who would carve the Queen's head to be stamped by the mint on British coins. When she has made the stamp it is reduced in size and then stamped on each coin. Lovingly and carefully she tries to reproduce a perfect likeness of Her Majesty. What a task! But of course, no human being can reproduce a perfect likeness, only God can. When God does a thing, he does it perfectly and in Jesus the stamp is exactly like himself. If you want to know what God is like, look at Jesus – that is the simple truth. There is nothing that Jesus is in personality that God isn't, and nothing that God is that Jesus isn't. He is the express image; he is, as the NIV has it, the exact representation. So we need be in no doubt now as to what God is like. He has not hidden himself, he has exposed his character for the whole world to see.

After three years, there was still one of the twelve disciples who said, "Show us the Father and we will be satisfied." Jesus said, "Oh Philip, have I been with you all this time and you still don't know who I am? Anyone who has seen me has seen the Father."

We are all made in the image of God and therefore, in some degree, every human being reflects something of that image. That is what we must remember when we look at the most degraded person. That is why murder – taking life maliciously, wilfully, deliberately – is wrong, and why euthanasia is wrong. The Bible teaches us that it is wrong because you are touching the image of God. I foretold many years ago that we were heading towards legalised euthanasia and we see that in some countries today. But in so many people the image has been so defaced that you can hardly see it any more. It is like an old, worn coin. I once gave my son an old coin and said, "I think it's very valuable. See if you can find out what it is." It was just a small lump of metal with marks on it. I said, "I think it's at least a thousand years old." But he found out it was two thousand years old, a coin from the Roman Republic. The image was almost gone, but once we knew what we were looking for, we could see a dolphin and a galley. Comparing it with a modern Italian coin bearing a dolphin and galley we could see the same image. That is how it is with people—when you meet them there is an image of God there, though sometimes you have to look very hard. It has been so spoiled by the deadly sins that mar us, but it is there. When you look at Jesus it is all there and of no other human being is this true. You can see exactly what God is like in Jesus.

What is God's relationship to his creatures, to humanity? What is Jesus' relationship to us? So far we have been thinking of his *revelation* and of *creation* through him, now we turn to his *redemption*.

What is he to you? A great man? An example? He is, but that doesn't even begin to describe him. There are just two things this verse states about Jesus—he is only these two things to believers not to unbelievers. He is a *Saviour* with a cross; and he is a *Lord* with a crown.

Let us take the first thing: "After he had provided purification for sins...." Do you realise that there is nobody else in the world who can do that for themselves or for anyone else? You try to deal with your besetting sin by yourself. Try to get somebody else to deal with it. There is no doctor, no psychiatrist, no scientist and no politician who can purify your life from sins. It is the hardest thing in the world to do. That is why it takes the Son of God to do it. He could only do it because he was the only man who has ever lived a perfect life himself and who could therefore offer it as a sacrifice and atonement for our imperfect lives. It says he did it *by himself* —that's emphasised, he had no help. If

41

I may say this: he not only had no help from men to do this but God left him to do it on his own. When he was doing it he cried, "My God, my God, why have you forsaken me?" By himself he made purification for sins.

Sins can be forgiven, blotted out and taken away. Nobody else can offer to do that for you because nobody else has provided what is needed for it. He is the Saviour with a cross. The priests of the Old Testament tried so hard to do it. They went through hundreds of thousands of bulls and goats. They went through it every year. They went through it every day and still they got nowhere nearer to getting purified. If they got pure then they would have finished the sacrifices but they never got pure so they had to keep on offering them.

Therefore, very importantly, every priest had to remain standing because his work was never done. He could never sit down and say "It's finished" because he knew the next day he would have to offer more sacrifices for more sins. But when Jesus made purification for sins he sat down at the right hand of God the Father. The expression "sat down" is full of meaning. You only sit down when your work is finished. Priests stood daily before the altar but he sat down, which brings us to the final point: *he is not only Saviour with a cross he is Lord with a crown*. Where is Jesus now? For the writer to the Hebrews there is emphasis here that when Christ rose from the dead that that was only the beginning of a journey in which he went on up; he rose, he came up from the dead but he didn't stop there. He went on up and he ascended through the clouds out of the sight of men. He went on up until he reached highest heaven and then he sat down. Where is Jesus now? He is in the throne room of the universe, at the right hand of God the Father. From there he supervises and controls what happens, not only on our planet earth, but he superintends the universe with its almost infinite spaces. He is in control, all authority in heaven and on earth is given to him, and there he sits today on the throne of the universe.

Nothing happens except by permission of Jesus, a carpenter from Nazareth. There is no more sublime statement of Jesus than these three verses. This is God's last word spoken all at once and once for all. He has no more word for us except to direct us to this Jesus. If we knew nothing more about Jesus than these verses, we would know enough. For in these verses we have Jesus portrayed as prophet ("God has spoken to us through his Son"), as priest ("he has made purification for sins") and as King ("he sat down at the right hand of God").

BETTER THAN ANGELS
Read 1:4 – 2:18

A. DID NOT SIT WITH ANGELS (1:4–14)
1. Son and his deity (5–6; 8–18) –worship and homage
2. Servants and their duty (7, 14) – winds and fire
B. DID NOT SPEAK BY ANGELS (2:1–4)
1. Direct message (3) – Lord and apostles
2. Distributed miracles (4) – signs and wonders
C. DID NOT SUFFER FOR ANGELS (2:5–18)
1. World subject to man (5–9) – glory and honour
    a. Ideal
    b. Actual
2. Man subject to death (10–18) – flesh and blood

I don't know if you have ever met an angel and perhaps neither do you either because you can entertain them unaware – when they materialise they can look just like human beings and they are a very real part of God's creation. Jews tend to think much more than Christians about angels. There is a very sound reason for that, so we shouldn't forget angels. The pages of the New Testament are full of their ministry. They are a higher order of beings than humans and they did not evolve from men. If you are stuck with the idea that all life must evolve and must come from simpler forms of life then you really have a problem with believing in angels.

But God created angels as a separate order of creation:

below him and above man. Therefore, they are between us and God—they are superior to us in intelligence, in beauty, in strength and in power. One day all believers will meet them. When you die, when your relatives and friends can no longer do anything for you or look after you as a person, though they may reverently look after your body, that moment the angels will take you to be in Abraham's bosom; that moment the angels will serve you. So we will meet them, and if the Lord comes again before you die then he is coming with all his angels so we will meet them that way. We worship God with angels and archangels and they watch a congregation and if one person in the congregation comes to Christ, the angels rejoice.

If a teacher misleads one of the little ones in the Sunday school, then the angel will report that back to heaven. Angels are terribly real. They are around us even though we don't normally see them. We can claim their protection. It is not just little children who can go to bed and claim the protection of angels while they sleep. The hosts of the Lord encamp around those who fear him. The Jews thought a great deal about the angels for the obvious reason that the angels were between them and God. When they saw God they saw him high and lifted up as Isaiah did. They felt the great gulf not only morally but physically. God was a long way off. They had to call on his name. He seems so far away in highest heaven. So they were glad that there was somebody in the gap in between. They were glad there were angels to bridge the gap.

When Isaiah saw the Lord high and lifted up – such a long way away it seemed – then came one of the angels with a live coal off the altar, right to Isaiah. It is as if the angel acts as the go-between, the mediator, and that was how the Jews thought of angels for that is what they did. When God had something to say to the Jews, he so often sent an angel.

When God gave the Ten Commandments he gave them first to the angels, then the angels gave them to Moses, and Moses passed them along to Israel.

It was therefore only a matter of time until the Jews began to ask: could the angels take messages back to heaven for us? They began to pray not to angels but through angels. So angels figured very largely in their thinking and in their experience too. Abraham met more than one. All through the Old Testament you find angels appearing and disappearing.

But you do in the New Testament too, in Jesus' life from his temptation right through to Gethsemane, and then again at the resurrection. The only crisis when angels were not present was his death. Jesus had a personal retinue of ten thousand of them who would do anything he commanded them. There are myriads of them altogether, but the personally assigned bodyguard for Jesus was ten thousand angels. They are there in the book of Acts, they are there opening prison doors and letting Peter out, they are there comforting Paul on his way to Rome, and if you read the last book of the Bible it is crammed with angels. So full of them it would fill the universe if it wasn't for the fact that there is space reserved for us too. The heavens are full of singing angels in the book of Revelation. Our worship here on earth is just a tiny echo of heavenly worship that is going on all the time. We are just joining in – the angels are not joining in with us; we are joining in with them. They are doing it all the time and we just come for an hour and a half or so, and we join with the angels and archangels and cry, "Holy, holy, holy...."

Jews thought a lot about them. So why then do Christians not think so much about them? Are we at fault here? Well, we are partly. I am afraid we have passed through an era in our day when we got so materialistic and naturalistic in our thinking, even within church, that we stopped thinking about angels. I was brought up in an era and in a church where they were never mentioned. I never thought about them. I found that when I preached about angels, it has been fresh material to people who have been going to church for years.

That is not the whole reason why we don't think so much about angels. It is because we have Jesus, and Jesus is better than any angels. He is at one stage called the covenant angel in the Bible, but he is more than an angel. The word "angel" simply means messenger. It doesn't necessarily mean wings and flowing robes. It means someone with something to say on behalf of someone else. We don't listen to angels speak to us now because we have got Jesus.

We are following the theme in Hebrews that Christianity is better than any other religion. To make the comparison, the writer takes the highest religion known until Jesus came and then he compares it with Jesus, and he is saying that Jesus is better every time. We saw the first contrast, which only took three verses. The old religion of the Jews was a religion of prophets who spoke the Word of God. It was in bits and pieces, and now we have a much better revelation of God. Now God speaks to us in his Son, not in fragments but in one whole – not in many forms but in one form, the form of a man.

Now we go back to that other link in the Old Testament chain of God speaking. God speaks to the angels who speak to the prophets who speak to the people. Now we are taking those two middle links and the first link we took was the prophets. We said Jesus is better than the prophets. Now we take the other link and we say Jesus is better than the angels. If you have Jesus, you are directly in touch with the Father; you are straight through. We don't need to pray through angels, we pray through Jesus Christ our Lord. That is maybe why angels don't figure as largely in our worship as they do in Jewish worship.

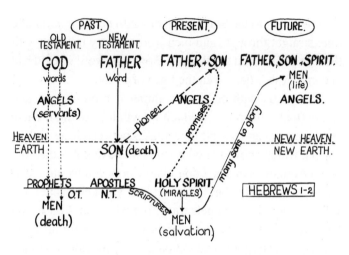

Now we are going to draw out this comparison. I want to do it by taking three periods of time. We are going to look at the present first, then at the past, and then the future — that is the order in the letter to the Hebrews.

See the diagram above. The left column is divided vertically into two parts: Old Testament and New Testament — both of which were written in the past and represent two phases of God's dealings with us in the past. Under phase one, notice the dotted lines coming down. They represent God speaking in bits and pieces to the Jews. You see that from God the dotted lines go down to angels, his servants, then they go further down to prophets, then they go down to men through the prophets and that is how God spoke in the Old Testament days.

Then notice the horizontal dotted line across the middle. Above it is heaven and below it is earth, and at the far right end it becomes the new heaven and the new earth. So God's Word came to earth in those stages — through the angels in heaven, to the prophets on earth, to the men, but in the New Testament there is a much simplified procedure. Now there is a solid line. It all came at once, not in bits and pieces, and it came direct to the Son of God on earth below that middle line: straight through, and men were directly in touch with the Son of God and the Word of God. The Word of God had become flesh – had taken the form of a man.

Connecting with the three columns is present, past, and future (that is the order in which we will look at this). There are three comparisons this letter makes between Jesus and the angels, which show that with Jesus we have got something better even than angels. I don't know how you would feel if when travelling by car, bus or on foot you knew that there were a whole lot of angels travelling with you. You would feel pretty important going along the street with all these angels protecting you and marching by your side. I will tell you something better — you go up the high street with Jesus and that's ten times better. Why is it better? There are three things said here about Jesus — one in the past, one in the present and one in the future. Firstly, Jesus did not sit with angels. Jesus does not sit with angels today. Secondly, in the past Jesus did not speak through angels; and, thirdly, in the future and you may find this a bit surprising at first but its main reference is future: Jesus did not suffer for angels. This puts angels very much in the second place.

Jesus did not sit with angels. A son does not sit with servants; they have separate tables. Go to Buckingham Palace and you will find many servants of the Queen. Though they sit in a palace they do not sit with the son of the Queen. It is not right that the son should be treated as a servant. That is why when the prodigal son came home and said, "Make me as one of your hired servants," that was out of the question. The father could never make the son sit with the servants.

Jesus is the Son of God, not just the servant. So when he ascended to highest heaven he sat down not with the angels but at the right hand of his Father. He doesn't sit with the servants. Would you rather know one of the servants in

Buckingham Palace or know the son? If you knew one of the servants it might give you access to one or two of the rooms, but if you knew the son you could get into every room. If you want total access to God, it is the Son you must know, not one of his servants.

Now the writer goes into the Old Testament. Remembering that he was addressing Jewish Christians may be a little strange to you. Do look up the references, go back into the Old Testament, see where they come from. Since the writer is talking to Jews he is going to use their scriptures. You should only really use the Bible towards those who will accept it. When the apostles preached to Jews they quoted scripture, when they preached to Gentiles they didn't. It's rather an important point this. You can't throw the Bible at someone who does not yet accept it. But when somebody says, "I believe it", then you can quote it. The Jews believed the Old Testament so this writer says, "I'm going to prove it from your own Old Testament." There is a lovely pattern here. Let me try to analyse it for you.

Eight things are given by way of contrast between Jesus and the angels. The pattern is this: three things about Christ, one about the angels; three things about Christ, one about the angels. You can see his prejudice can't you, and it's a good one—three words about Christ to one about anybody else. But those two quadruple quotes make up eight altogether. It is as if we go twice through this pattern and are given three texts from the Old Testament that tell you Jesus is Son, and one to tell you angels are servants; three more to tell he is Son; one more to tell you angels are servants, and this really puts them in their place.

Let me draw the total contrast: the Son and his deity; the angels and their duty—that is the contrast. It separates them out in our thinking so that we never put Jesus among the angels. We see him high above them all, and the angels simply as ministering spirits — at the moment above us but, as we shall see, one day to be beneath us, and we will be above the angels one day—not just with them but above them. They will come and ask you for their orders for the day. Can you imagine that? You may never have had the privilege or opportunity of having a servant on earth, but you will have them in heaven — not just a room in heaven but a room with a servant to match. Are you looking forward to glory or do you find the whole idea a little embarrassing? Well, you won't. They will be such wonderful ministering spirits that you will love the service they render to you.

We will now run through the text. Psalm 2 is referred to and it is simply a psalm to point out that God never said to an angel, "You are my son. Today I've become your father." People have debated much about what the "today" means. I believe it means the eternal day of God, God's today, not any point in time but God's today. That's always for God as the great *I am*—today. It doesn't matter what day it is. Is it the day of Christ's birth? Is it the day of his ascension? Is it the day of his resurrection? They are all included in this "today". It does not matter what today it is, today God is Father, Jesus is Son. Angels are called, "sons of God" but they are never called *the* "Son" (with a capital "S"). That is never used as a name whereas "Jesus" is a name – Son. The Father says, "This is my Son. I am so pleased with him."

Next there is 2 Samuel 7—originally applied to Solomon, but because Solomon was the son of David who will build God's house, he becomes a kind of foreshadowing of another Son of David for whom the word said to Solomon would be even more true. You are my Son; I'll be your Father.

Thirdly, there is Psalm 97 — and when Christ came into the world the angels had to worship him. When does this refer to? Again scholars are divided but I think it is best to tell you of two things they think, and that both are right.

When Jesus came to this planet the first time, the angels in heaven looked down at the little baby and they worshipped. But when he comes a second time the angels will be there again and they will worship him again, so we should never bow down before the angels. We should only worship Christ.

In the book of Revelation, John twice made the mistake of bowing down and worshipping an angel. Frankly, if you saw an angel you would be tempted to bow down and worship. If an angel came in real glory and you realised that this was a supernatural visitor from another world, from heaven itself, and you had an angel in your home, you would tend to fall on your knees. But if you did, the angel would lift you up and say, "Don't worship me. Worship Christ." The next quote is the first one about the angels after three about the Messiah, the Christ. This one says, "God has made the angels." Now that word is never used of Jesus. He is the only-begotten Son but he was not *made*. To be *made* means to be created. To be made means that once you did not exist, now you do.

The angels were made and that word is never used of the Son of God. So he did not become the Son of God at a certain point in time. He always was the Son of God, the only-begotten Son of God, "Begotten not made". But the angels were made. God made the angels ministering spirits, servants to do his will. They do it through the powers of nature sometimes—wind and fire, which can be the sign of an angel moving. I think that is what disturbed the waters of a pool mentioned in the Gospels—a ministering spirit stirred up the waters, and an angel was doing it.

The next four quotes are concerned more with what is done. Psalm 45 says a wonderful thing. At the coronation of Queen Elizabth II, a straight ornamented sceptre was placed in her hands. A symbol of an unjust reign is a crooked sceptre, but the symbol of justice has to be straight. Then she was anointed on the head with olive oil, the chrism. These two things are said here in a psalm about Jesus – that God said to him: you are not only eligible to be King, you are capable of being King. Alas, those two things don't always go together. If you study English history you will find that there have been kings and queens who were eligible but not capable. They may have been a son or a daughter of royalty and they came to the throne, but they proved on the throne that they were not fit to rule. Other kings and queens in history not only have been eligible but capable. Jesus is not only eligible because he is Son of God, he is capable because he loves righteousness and hates wickedness.

I want you to notice that you are not a truly good person until you hate wickedness as well as love righteousness. I find there are plenty of people in the world who love goodness, but you do not find that they hate evil. True goodness is composed of both those sides. True righteousness has a positive and a negative aspect. A man may love good people and may love goodness, and still not be truly upright in God's sight. A truly upright man is a man who hates evil when he sees it. So God says to Jesus, "You have loved righteousness, you have hated wickedness, therefore here is the sceptre and here is the anointing with oil. I crown you as King and your throne will last for ever and ever." The King of the universe today is Jesus. All authority in heaven and earth is given to him and he sits there on the throne, a throne which he will have forever and ever, and he sits there with a straight sceptre in his hand, the oil on his forehead. Because when he was on earth he loved righteousness and hated wickedness—that has never been said to an angel.

Psalm 102 is the next quote. Here again we go back to the first three verses of chapter 1 in thought: Christ, as the Creator, he made it all and one day he will wrap it all up. It is a lovely phrase. Sometimes the translators have translated it like pulling the curtains. You look up at the heavens, see the stars, and one day they will just be pulled away, as you opened your curtains when you got up this morning. Others have said: you will roll them up like old clothes. You have worn many different clothes in your lifetime. Have you ever worked out how many? And when they were worn out you bundled them up and away they went. This is the picture here: like a worn-out garment. This universe is wearing out.

Once, for a little mental relaxation, I was trying to read a book on Einstein's Theory of Relativity. Though it is written for beginners, I just began to grasp it. I learned some fascinating facts. I learned that the stars were all wearing themselves out and the sun is burning itself up. It is only a matter of time until it is all burned up, all worn out. We are in a changing universe and only Jesus is changeless. All the universe is wearing out. But Jesus is responsible for those changes and he will roll it all up like a garment, like a worn out suit of clothes. He will still be there. No angel is like that.

Psalm 110, "Sit here," says God, "at my right hand, until all your enemies are your footstool." An archeologist dug up from an ancient Egyptian tomb a footstool for a throne and on it were painted the faces of all the kings that man had conquered, so whenever he sat down had the satisfaction of looking down between his feet and seeing that. It was a vivid picture and it was the habit of the ancient world that when you defeated somebody you painted their face where you put your feet—they were under your feet. "Sit here until I make all your enemies your footstool." He has never said that to an angel.

So having said three more wonderful things about Christ he goes back to something else about the angels. Are they not all ministering spirits sent to serve whom? Christ? God? No, sent to serve believers, those who are to inherit salvation — the angels are sent to serve *you*. They are your servants. That is remarkable. That is why they are so thrilled when you become a Christian. They can begin their service to you because they are terribly afraid that if you don't become a Christian the service they will have to render is to God and it will be a ministry of judgment to you. Now that is the first main point. Not only did Jesus not sit with angels, he did not speak through angels.

Hebrews is very practical. It is full of warnings and the first four verses of chapter two are a serious warning. It is this: if we have so much better a message than the Jews ever had, and they were punished for ignoring the message they got, how much more will we be? Greater privilege brings greater responsibility. How much better is our message than theirs? Very simply—their message from God came through the angels, through the prophets, to them. It was third-hand by the time they got it. We got it firsthand. The message came in the shape of the Lord, the Word made flesh. The prophets witnessed to the old message, apostles have witnessed to the new message, and they not only gave us the message, they gave us miracles to prove the message was true. Wherever the true message is preached, God confirms the word with signs following, and things happen and you have a double testimony. You not only have the word of the gospel from firsthand witnesses who saw Jesus and heard him speak, you have miracles of the Holy Spirit, gifts of the Holy Spirit to confirm the truth of what has been said. You have got it visually; you have got it audibly. You have heard the message that we have both ways. The Jews never got the message in this way. Therefore, and I tremble to say this, it is the first terrible thing said in the letter to the Hebrews: there is nothing you need do to be damned except ignore this message. It is the only thing you need do. You don't need to have done wicked things, you don't need to have said a single wrong word, the only thing you need to do to go to hell after hearing this message is to ignore it—that is all.

Consider that! ***There must be thousands heading for hell in England — on no other ground then that they neglected such a great salvation.*** God took all that trouble — he not only sent angels and prophets in the past, but now he has sent his own Son and confirmed that word with miracles so you have no excuse for doubting its truth, and you deliberately ignore it or just drift away. Now here is a nautical term—the letter to the Hebrews was written by a man who had done a lot of sailing. He keeps bringing in nautical terms and the one used here is "drift away". It means not to have an anchor down, and just float along towards the rocks. A man who doesn't put his anchor down and just basks in the sun on the deck of his ship and lets it drift towards the rocks is a man who is an absolute fool. But most people go to hell by drifting there, not by deciding to go there. They go there because they have had a chance to get an anchor firm to the rock and they don't put their anchor overboard, they don't get linked on to the truth. They listen, they are interested, and then they forget it and just drift away — just neglect, apathy and indifference.

A doctor I knew said, "I was invited to go to speak to a youth club in the Midlands. I gave my talk and they just met it with stony indifference. All the way home I was really worried. I prayed, 'Lord, is there something wrong with me? Was that a dull address?'"

He was really worried, thinking his speaking days might be over. He didn't get through at all. But the next week he was invited in London to speak to a group of nurses and young people from Thailand, and he decided to give the same address. He said, "This time it just really went over. I realise that they were hungry; that they had got an appetite; that they couldn't get enough of God's Word. It was the same address and I was so relieved that it wasn't me."

Same address — but in one case no appetite, neglect,

indifference; in the other case soaking it up. Here the letter to the Hebrews says this, "If Jesus is so much better than the angels, how shall we escape if we neglect what is so much better?" You see, in the Old Testament nobody was punished for neglecting or ignoring the message. They were punished only for direct contradiction of it in life. They were punished for disobedience. They were punished for transgression but not for ignoring it. But in fact in the New Testament it is more serious. There is a specific punishment here of eternal lost-ness to those who just ignore, to those who hear and drift away, to those who never put an anchor of faith into this truth, to those who just let it slide, Sunday after Sunday, week after week, month after month, year after year, without even realising that they are drifting straight towards the rocks and disaster. That is all you need do to go to hell.

If Jesus is better than the angels and people were punished for disobeying the angels, how shall we escape if we neglect? You know perfectly well if you neglect your garden what will happen to it. You know perfectly well if you neglect the paintwork on your house what will happen to it. You know perfectly well if you neglect your health what will happen to it. Then how will you escape if you neglect so great a salvation? Isn't it strange that people can apply commonsense to every other department of life but their souls, and can neglect that and drift on as if it will all turn out right in the end? That is the second contrast and it is a serious one. The first contrast: he did not sit with angels. Second, he didn't speak through angels. Third contrast, he did not suffer for angels.

God has decreed that everything is to be subject to man. He has decreed it and that decree has never been cancelled and it will be fulfilled. Now science is feeling after the fulfilment of that decree, and a scientist cannot help going on to discover. We sometimes ask — should scientists have discovered something? But a scientist can't help it. I have done a bit of science and I know that once you are on to something you want to find out about it. It is almost like a drug—you have got to know, you can't just stop. You are searching for man's conquest of things. So our scientific discoveries are a partial fulfilment of this text that God has decreed that everything shall be subject to man.

When we conquer space as we reach out in our puny way to a tiny little corner of space, we are partially fulfilling this text. We are subjecting something new to man. Think of God's decree and the ideal. We have been made just a little lower than the angels. What is man that you care for him? What is man that you think about him? You made him just a little lower than the angels. You have given him dominion over everything.... That is what God said in Genesis: "Let them have dominion...." Science has increasingly put man in charge of something. Let everything be subject to man. That is the ideal.

But I have said science is only a partial fulfilment, because if there is one thing that science is saying it is that things are getting on top of us. I don't need to underline the fact of pollution just to give you one illustration of this. It seems as if we can control everything but ourselves, and that is a real handicap to science. For it means that almost every scientific discovery there has been of any major kind has been used to destroy as well as to save. Things are getting on top of us now and we are wondering just how long we can go on living on this little spaceship called the earth. The air is running out, the fresh water is running out, we just wonder how long we can keep going. We don't yet see all things in subjection to man. It is an ideal that has not come true even with all our science. 75% of all the scientists of history are alive today—such has been the growth in scientific knowledge. Knowledge is doubling every ten years and it will soon double every five years. We are trying to get all things into subjection to ourselves but we can't even feed the mouths of the people on earth yet, and we can't stop war yet. We can only make it more scientific. So we don't see the ideal in the actual. What do we see then? We see man fighting a losing battle against things.

But we see Jesus as the pioneer of the fulfilment of this decree. We see in heaven a Man who is above all things. We see a Man who was made like us a little lower than the angels but who is now way above them. We see a Man in charge of the universe, and already this decree has been fulfilled in the case of the one Man, Jesus, who is over everything. Now this was not true of Jesus before he was born because he was not then a man. He was the Son of God. So if he had been on that throne before he was born you could not say that all things were subject to man. But we do see now one who is made a little lower than the angels now high above them, now controlling all things, and so it is true for one man so far. Now here is the glorious truth: it is going to be true of hundreds of thousands of others. You see, Jesus has conquered all of known space. Therefore he can move freely around the universe. Look at the efforts we make just to take a tiny (we say it's a giant leap) leap into space. Giant leap? It is a fleabite compared to the distance of space, a tiny step. It is not a giant leap, but Jesus just stepped out without a space suit, right out into space, into the universe, and one day you and I will travel the entire universe.

People ask me where there will be room in heaven for us. If there is a new universe and you can travel anywhere in it, that won't be a problem. Think of it—all things subject to us. We know that even in his lifetime this was true of Jesus. He could speak to the wind and the waves. He could turn water into wine. He could multiply loaves and fishes—one day that power will be yours. The universe will be subject to man. Won't science look silly then? It really will. It will look like a child in a kindergarten trying to build bricks, compared to the day when all things are subject to man.

Now we come to the close of this theme. You see the world, the universe, subject to man—that's God's decree. He wants us to be in complete control of all that he has made and he never gave that to angels. It is man who is to be in charge of the universe. We already see one Man in charge of it and we are going to join him and many sons will come to glory and share his control. That is what we are looking forward too, but now we come to the serious side. Why can science not do this for us? Because science can only see the mental need, it cannot see the moral need. Do you see the difference? Science says: if we will only apply our mental facilities we can get in charge of everything, we can subject everything to ourselves. No you can't, scientist. You are ignoring the moral factor. You have got to learn to control yourself before you can control everything else.

Jesus came to earth to be made flesh and blood, a little lower than the angels, that he might be the first man to get above them again, and to take control of the universe. In this he is our pioneer. That is the word used here—the one who blazes the trail, who goes first and prepares the way for others—the pioneer of our salvation. He came to earth not only to become man that he might take over the universe as man, he came that he might die and put men right morally as well as mentally. He came to deliver them from something that no man can control—death.

The fear of death strikes even the scientist's heart. Every scientist dies, every great man dies. However much we achieve — we may stand on the moon but we will become dust on the earth. This bondage, the one fact of our existence which we cannot get on top of, is due to the fact that there is something else we can't control either, and that is sin.

For death is the result of sin. If we are going to control the universe, somebody had to come and deal with those two things. Somebody had to come, and not only become man, they had to be exposed to all the horrible pressure of temptation. Only a sinless man could know the awful pressure that there can be of wanting to do something wrong. We only feel it to a degree because we are sinners. The holier you get, the greater the pressure of temptation. Make no mistake. You start as an unbeliever and you don't feel the pressure very much. You become a Christian and you begin to feel the pressure a bit more. You get nearer to Christ, the pressure of temptation gets fiercer. This is a proof to you that those who can sympathise most with sinners are not those who have sinned but those who have been sinless and been tempted. Can you see that? We often think that if I sin I can sympathise most with someone who is struggling with that same sin. Not at all! On the other hand, if I have never been tempted with that sin, I can't sympathise either. The person who can sympathise most with a person under temptation and who is sinning is a person who has felt all the force of that particular temptation but has not sinned. Isn't that right? They know the pressure more than anyone else. That one is our Jesus.

We were all our lifetime in the grip of one big fear of one thing we can't control—death. We can put it off for a bit but we can't stop it. No scientist in the world has yet discovered any way of controlling death —because we haven't discovered any way of controlling sin. That is because we weren't saved, and that is why the key word here is not the word "angels", though it occurs about twelve times, but the word "salvation", which occurs in each of the three sections of our study. The world is to be subject to man, but unfortunately man is subject to death. Who can break through? The Son of God has broken through. No angel died for us and Jesus did not die for the angels.

That is the other side of this truth. Angels have sinned, one-third of them have sinned, and therefore forfeited their right to go on living in heaven. But none of them will benefit from the death of Jesus. When an angel, who has lived in heaven in the presence of God, sins, then there is no alternative but for that angel to go to hell with the devil. But with man, who has not lived in heaven, God sent his only Son to earth not just to become man but to be tempted and become a great high priest and lift us up and bring many sons to glory, and set us above the angels and in charge of the universe. That is my future in Jesus Christ, and it is yours too if you know him. If you don't know him and neglect and ignore this truth, you will not finish up on the throne of the universe in control of everything, you finish up in hell with everything on top of you—that is the alternative, and it is your decision which it shall be.

Behind all this is God, "For whom and through whom everything exists." Now we believe the "through whom," but we often forget the "for whom". You are not here for yourself; you are here for God.

You are not here that God may bless your purposes and plans; you are here that you may do his purposes and plans. You are not here primarily to enjoy God; you are here that God may enjoy you.

"For whom all things exist"; "To bring many sons to glory" — is not glory for me, it is glory for God. That is what he made you for.

People ask why God made man. The answer is very simple: he wanted a larger family. When Jesus came to earth, those he got hold of he was not ashamed to call brothers.

3

BETTER THAN MOSES AND JOSHUA
Read 3:1 – 4:13

A. MOSES – OUT OF EGYPT (3:1–19)
1. Faithful house (1–6)
      a. Moses – in – servant
      b. Jesus – over – son
      c. We – of – sons (stones)
2. Faithless hearts (7–19)
      a. What? (7–11)
      b. When? (12–15)
      c. Who? (16–19)
B. JOSHUA – INTO CANAAN (4:1–13)
1. Disobedient works (1–10)
      a. Seventh day (3–5)
      b. Certain day (6–8)
      c. Sabbath day (9–10)
2. Discerning word (11–13)
      a. Down
      b. In
      c. Out

Now we are going to draw the comparison between Jesus and two pioneers, two of the greatest leaders of the Old Testament: Moses and Joshua. Moses got the people out of Egypt; Joshua got them into Canaan, with forty years in between. Jesus is better than Moses and he is better than Joshua for reasons we are going to see in a moment. So even the greatest people in the Old Testament pale into insignificance when they are placed alongside Jesus.

Notice that chapter 3 addresses us as holy brethren with a heavenly calling. Straight away that puts Christians in a category different from Jews. Jews called each other "brethren" and they regarded themselves as brethren, but they were not *holy* brethren; they were no saints; whereas in the New Testament every Christian is described as a saint. We are holy brethren. Furthermore, Israel, the Jews, had a calling from God but it was an earthly calling to possess a land which you can draw in an atlas or on the globe of the world. We are *holy* brethren, not just brethren, and we have a *heavenly* calling, not just a calling. It is a calling to a heavenly country, which is even more wonderful. So straight away those two adjectives place Christians above Jews. When you know the Old and the New Testaments, it is these tiny differences that make all the difference. Just adjectives tell you we have moved into a new dimension of spirituality.

The address to these holy brethren with a heavenly calling is that they should do more than *confess* Jesus, they should *consider* him. That may be one of the reasons why we don't get on too far with Jesus. It is not enough just to confess him, *consider* whom you confess. The word "consider" means to give such earnest attention; to think so hard about something that you get the message, that you discover the hidden meaning. Or, as one person has put it, that you master the mystery. So Christ said, "Consider the lilies...." Take the flowers in your garden. Don't just look at them. Don't just say, "Haven't I got a lovely garden" or, "Aren't those flowers lovely?" *Consider* the lilies, look at them until you get their meaning, until you get their message: God clothes them beautifully, he will look after you. But there are many people who go to a flower show and never consider flowers; they never get the message. You can confess Jesus and wear a Jesus sticker badge and say, "I belong to Jesus and I'm not ashamed to confess him." But have you *considered* him? Do you *think* about him? Do you try and master the mystery? Do you look at Jesus with such fixed attention that you get the message—so that you understand who he is and what he can do for you? Plenty of people confess Jesus, but not so many consider him and think about him and meditate and understand.

Now we are to consider him in two of his capacities: *apostle* and *high priest*. When did you last consider that Jesus was one of the apostles? Perhaps you have never considered that. Well now, let's consider that. Jesus is an apostle. What does that mean? In simple modern language, a *missionary*, for the word "apostle" in Greek simply means to be *sent*.

When the Greek was rendered in Latin, they used the word *mittere* which means to send. From that come our words "missile", "mission", "missionary", and a whole lot of other things that mean "sent". A missile is sent out from earth and up into the heavens. Jesus was a missionary from the heavens to earth. Do you realise that?

All Christian missionary work takes its inspiration from his first missionary visit to this planet. "As the Father has sent me..." in the Greek: "As the Father apostled me, so I apostle you," so I send you. I was sent; I send you. Do you consider Christ as the *sent* one? As the one to whom the Father said, "I send you to planet earth to help those of my children down there. You will have to leave home, you will have to become a missionary. You will have to leave all the glory that you have been accustomed to, all that you have had by way of service as the Son of God. You will have to go and become a servant. Will you go? Will you be sent? The Lord Jesus was the supreme sent one who said, "Here am I. Send me" —and he came.

So we are going to consider Jesus as the one who was sent to help. Moses was one sent to help, Joshua was sent to help, and God is looking for people whom he can send to help someone else. Moses and Joshua were sent to do a specific job, and where they failed, Jesus succeeded. For they were both sent for one purpose: to bring God's people to rest. Moses didn't achieve it and Joshua didn't achieve it. Moses didn't achieve it because out of two and a half million he got out of Egypt, he only got two into Canaan and the rest perished on the way. Joshua didn't succeed, and though he got them into Canaan, which was to be the land of rest, they did not have rest in that land. The reasons come out in the book of Joshua. Moses and Joshua as sent ones failed not just because of themselves but because of the people's reaction to their leadership. But then came Jesus with his invitation: "Come to me all who labour and are heavy laden and I will give you rest." He got people out of Egypt and into Canaan. It is he who brings rest to our souls.

Let's look at Moses and Joshua. Incidentally, it is interesting that the names "Joshua" and "Jesus" are exactly the same name. In fact, in the Authorized Version of Hebrews 4:8 there is a bad mistake: where it meant Joshua, the AV has Jesus. If you have a Bible with that in, cross it out and write in "Joshua". It is a comparison between Joshua and Jesus though it is the same name. Chapter 3 is about Moses and how he got the people out of Egypt. Chapter 4 is about how Joshua got them into Canaan — and both chapters are about how Moses and Joshua failed to bring them rest. That is why Christianity is superior. Judaism does not bring people rest, it makes them labour and become heavy laden with all the burdens that Judaism imposes. ***Christianity brings rest because it tells a person to stop trying and start trusting.***

Moses was great but Jesus is greater. Moses was faithful, there is no question about that. He had stick-ability, that unique quality which makes a man a leader: the ability to go on when nobody else will go on; the ability to remain loyal when everybody else is unfaithful. Moses did a good job. Time and again he pleaded with God for the people and he stayed with them. He could have washed his hands of them. But he was so faithful to his people that he said, "Lord, if you're going to blot them out you can blot me out as well. I'm going to stay with them," and God honoured that faithfulness. Jesus also was faithful — in having loved his own, he loved them to the end. That sort of fidelity is vital in leadership.

But there is a difference between Moses and Jesus. Moses was faithful as a servant is faithful. Jesus was faithful as a son is faithful. There is a big difference between an employee and a son being faithful. There is a greater degree of voluntary fidelity with a son. In a sense, a servant has extra sanctions from outside to be faithful in a job. But a son is free, and a son being faithful is a wonderful thing, more wonderful than a servant. More than that, Moses was in God's house whereas Jesus built it. There is always a big difference between a person who lives in the house compared with a person who built it for himself to inhabit. Actually, the house I live in was built by a builder for himself to live in. There were other employees who worked on it I have no doubt, but the builder built it for himself. That put him in a totally different relationship to the house than that of those who actually did the plastering, and it is very well built as you might imagine.

Moses was simply a servant in God's house. Jesus, the Son, was the builder of the house and built it for himself to inhabit, so there is again almost no comparison between the two. You can see the gulf between Moses and Jesus already.

When we say "God's house" we are not referring to a building of bricks and mortar, timber or stone. We are referring to people, as we talk about the royal family; our Queen is of the "house" of Windsor. Here the word "house" means the house of Israel; the household; the family. So Hebrews is saying that Moses was part of the house, part of that which was built, whereas Jesus was the one who built that which was built, and inhabits that which was built, and lives in his people. Hebrews says, "You are that house" and this is one of the most exciting thoughts. I once tried to get across this meaning to a Sunday school class. To test the children to see if they understood, I said, "If somebody asks you tomorrow morning where is the church, the house of God, what will you say?" A little girl replied, 'I will say I'm it.'" Consider this: you are the house, and we are servants in the house like Moses, but there's a Son of the house who built it and who inhabits it.

Moses failed to build a restful house. How important that is. Have you noticed that in some houses you can relax and in some you can't? It is awfully difficult to find out why. Some houses maybe are just so ideal home-ish that you feel like an intruder, and that you would spoil a photograph of the living room! But it is not just that. In some houses people can create rest so that when you go in you can relax, though other homes are tense. However beautiful the home, the tension is there; you can't relax because there isn't reality there. Moses, though faithful in God's house, did not bring rest to it. In fact, very often there was a real tension between Moses and others in the house. Again, the fault was in the people. Moses was a great leader. He knew exactly where he was going. God had revealed everything he needed to know. People accepted him at first, but there came points where they would not accept his leadership, and real differences arose between Moses and the rest of God's house. Moses was the best leader that they could have asked for. What went wrong? The answer is that although it was a faithful house as far as Moses was concerned, it was full of faithless hearts as far as the people were concerned. What he said to them was not matched with faith in what he said. As we see in chapter 4, a message you hear from the Word of God can be of no value to you whatsoever if it isn't combined with faith in your heart; if you don't believe it (which means if you don't practise it), if you don't follow it through and trust and obey.

It went wrong in people's *hearts*. Four times the word, "heart" appears in the rest of the chapter — in the inside, it wasn't anything to do with the outside of them. The "heart" in scripture is a word that covers affections, thoughts, and motivation. It doesn't just mean the emotional side; it means everything *inside*, as we talk about the heart of a cabbage, meaning simply the very inner part. Something went wrong in the people's hearts, deep down inside. It wouldn't appear at first. When it was happening nobody might know it was happening. It may be happening in your heart this moment. You are either believing what I write here and responding to it and your life is going to be changed, or that heart is getting harder. We talk about people getting "gospel hardened". One of the reasons I don't preach a simple gospel sermon every Sunday is precisely that — many in a congregation would get "gospel hardened". If you rub a piece of skin and keep on rubbing it, that skin will get harder and harder. That is the word used here of hearts that get hard, calloused, they have heard it so often and nothing can penetrate. Today, if you hear his voice, harden not your hearts as they did in the wilderness. There is a reference here to two events in those forty years from Egypt to Canaan — one right at the beginning of the forty years, one right at the end to show that they did it for forty years. Every day they did it, all the way through. There was this hardness building up in their hearts. The first was at a place called Massah, which means provocation, and the second was at a place called Meribah, meaning temptation.

This is so true to our own hearts. It is very sad, isn't it? They were a people who had seen miracles, who had seen a Red Sea parted, who had seen water from a rock, who had been led forty years without their shoes wearing out in that wilderness of Sinai – and believe me, a normal pair of shoes would wear out in weeks in that climate. They had bread delivered daily from heaven to their tents (work out the millions of tons of manna that involved) and birds to eat, quails that almost flew into their hands. Having seen all these miracles, they say, "Why did you bring us out of Egypt?" Have you ever been tempted to say to God, "Why did you ever convert me? Why did you ever bring me out of sin? Why didn't you leave me alone? Why did you bring me into this weary pilgrimage?" That's what went wrong.

Scripture gives us this as a warning to us in our day. It is not whether you begin the Christian pilgrimage it is whether you continue and complete that matters. If you would have God's rest, just to start out doesn't bring rest. Indeed, there is a striving that must follow, to enter into rest. Is that a paradox? Strive to rest—it sounds like a contradiction, like trying to get yourself to sleep! In the pilgrimage to rest there is a striving, a struggling to get through to the promised land. There is a rough patch or desert, and every Christian has been through that desert to get through to rest. It is a struggle in the heat and burden of the day to keep going, but you know there is rest waiting and you are determined to get into it.

So Moses called the people of Israel to rest but they rebelled. They said, "Why did you start us on this journey?" When did they do it? Now here is an interesting point, which the letter makes—*today*. That is when we do it. That is when we harden our hearts. You don't do it yesterday, you don't do it tomorrow, you do it in the little patch of time that we call "today". This suddenly becomes relevant because this quotation from scripture is introduced with these words: so as the Holy Spirit says. Notice that what scripture says, the Holy Spirit says. So you can either say "the Bible says" or "the Spirit says" and you can say it about the same word. But notice that the word "says" is in the continuous present. Not "said," but "says". "Today," the Holy Spirit says, "if you hear his voice don't harden your heart; don't shut it out." It is *today* we have to make our decisions. You can't make decisions yesterday, that is as fixed as anything in the universe and more so, for you can change the universe, but you can't change yesterday. You can't decide tomorrow. Tomorrow isn't here. The only point at which you can respond to God as you should is *today* and the Holy Spirit says, "Today when you hear his voice...."

This is the time to respond. What you do with your todays decides whether you develop a hard heart, not what you do with your yesterdays or your tomorrows.

When David wrote this psalm it was already hundreds of years after Moses had called the people of Israel and they hardened their hearts. "Today" is the moment of truth—the moment when you either have a softened heart, which is melting and more responsive, more sensitive to the Holy Spirit's words, or you go away hardened. It went wrong in their "today" and it goes wrong in our "today".

We should encourage one another daily because today doesn't last forever. One day there will be only yesterdays. We can prevent each other getting hard by noticing when someone is beginning to do so and going to speak to them. It is a duty we have to each other, to be watching not just our own hearts but the hearts of our brethren. The heart gets hard first but it comes out in people's faces later. They can sit in a church looking like granite. If you notice that, encourage one another and help one another. "If we hold firmly till the end, the confidence we had at first...." The whole letter to the Hebrews is saying this: are you persevering with Christ?

Have you got as much confidence now as you had when you first came to him? Have you kept up the courage and hope? Are you still as firm in the faith? Are you holding on? Because it's not just having come out of Egypt, it's holding on to the promised land and going hard after it, knowing there is a rest ahead of you, that you have a goal. That will keep you sharing in Christ and able to minister to one another.

The next question is this: what went wrong? Unbelief led to disobedience, led to rebellion, destruction and failure to enter rest. When did it go wrong? It went wrong in their "today", and it goes wrong in our today. Who was all this about? Verse 16—everybody who came out of Egypt, which means in Christian language that every Christian is concerned with this. It is the *Christian* whose heart can be hardened. The Christian who has got out of Egypt, who has come out of Satan's slavery, who has been delivered from the kingdom of darkness – his or her heart can get hard, rebellious, critical, grumbling. So, brethren, let us be afraid lest we fall into the hands of the living God.

Did you know that God swears? That "today" when they rebelled, God took an oath. We can only take an oath by something or someone above ourselves, and God cannot do that because there is no-one above him, so he swears by himself. When God swears he says, "By myself I have sworn." On the day they rebelled, God swore on an oath because he was angry, but wouldn't you be angry? Don't you think that's a righteous anger? Don't you think he was justified? Having brought them out of Egypt, having sent Moses to them, having delivered them by miracle after miracle, they had no cause to complain. They had enough food, they had enough clothes, they were on their way to the promised land, yet still they grumbled – "Why did you take us out of Egypt? Why did you start us on this journey?"

No wonder God was angry, and so he swore, "By God

I will not share my rest with you." This whole passage is saying that God could look into your heart today and say, "By God I will not share my rest with him or with her." That would be a terrible tragedy. If your heart were to be hardening at this moment, you are tempting God to swear and to say that about you, and you will go back into a world in which you will have no final rest and in which, when you come to die, if they put "Rest in peace" on your tombstone it will be a lie. For God swears that those who rebel and refuse to believe the truth when they hear and see it will just not share his rest. Why should they? They would spoil it.

Now in chapter 4 we come to Joshua. Moses didn't get any of them into Canaan himself because he died. But two people went in – Joshua and Caleb – and they took in with them a whole group of people who had been born in the wilderness, so a new generation came into the land of Israel. Did they have rest? Read the books of Joshua and Judges. Read 1 and 2 Samuel and 1 and 2 Kings. Did they have rest? – Never! One of the tragedies of Israel is precisely that they still think, three thousand years after this, that if they can get to the promised land they will have rest, and they are fooled. They got to the promised land, and in 1948 the State of Israel was declared. They thought, "Now we can have rest from our enemies." Have they? Four major wars occurred in the following twenty-five years.

Rest is not just a place, is it? Many people are looking around the West Country for a retirement bungalow by the sea where they can have a permanent holiday. They think, "If only I could get a nice pension and get everything settled, I could have rest." Don't you believe it—there is no rest outside of God.

Rest is not just to be in the promised land but to be enjoying the promises. It is not just the promised land that they failed to reach, it is the land of promises they failed to reach. That land can be in any geographical location. You could go to Israel now and not enjoy any of the promises of God. You can stay in your home town and live in the land of promises.

That was the mistake they made and they still make it. They still hope that just being there in their own land will bring them rest, but it doesn't. Joshua therefore got them into Canaan but he didn't get them into rest. Says the letter to the Hebrews: "You should be mortally afraid of missing out on rest because you could do." I am addressing this to Christians now. You should have a healthy fear, having started the Christian life, that you shouldn't die before you enter into rest. So often we think of rest as something following death, but the Bible is offering us a rest *before* death – that you should cease from your own works before death, that you should be set free from yourself before death. So many people just don't enjoy that. The more they try to get it, the worse it becomes.

Why did they fail to enter rest? How do we fail to arrive? It all happened because twelve spies went into the promised land and came back carrying great bunches of grapes. (The tourist board of Israel's symbol is two spies carrying a bunch of grapes on a pole between them.) They came back and said, "It's great; it's everything we could have wished for. There are valleys, lush valleys full of grass, land flowing with milk and honey — look at these grapes, that's the land God has promised us." "But," said ten of the twelve, "there are cities with big walls and big people inside them and we will never make it." Joshua and Caleb alone said, "Yes we can. God is with us," but the other ten said, "No we can't," and the two and a half million with them said, "No we can't, we don't believe it."

God told Moses to turn them around — off you go back into the wilderness, and off they went, and it was years before they got back in, before they came anywhere near the borders again. This can happen to Christians. You see, this is a warning given to Christians today, not just to Jews then. You can get as near the promised land of rest as that, and then because you don't believe it can be yours you are condemned to spend the rest of your days in that kind of wilderness which is a halfway house, neither Egypt nor Canaan, and you are wandering for the rest of your life. There are Christians who die miserable because they never get into the promised land, because they have never found this rest. They are not enjoying the promises of God and they remain perpetual wilderness wanderers. It doesn't mean God deserts them. He still leads them, but in the wilderness rather than in the land.

So there are two sorts of Christians: there are carnal Christians who are still being led in the wilderness, and there are spiritual Christians who are being led in the land. God's purpose for every one of us is not just to get us out but to get us in. Not just to cut the wrong things out of your life but to put the right things in, for he wants you to enjoy him forever. If you are in the wilderness, that is a miserable Christian life because you are neither enjoying the pleasures of sin for a season in Egypt nor are you enjoying the pleasure of God's promises. That explains why some Christians are just so miserable. They set out but they didn't get there. They started but they didn't finish.

Now let's look at this matter of the *rest* of God. Do you realise that God is having a rest every day? Do you envy him? Well you can enjoy that rest. That doesn't mean that he is doing nothing. If that is your idea of rest, forget it. The Bible idea of rest is not doing nothing. God is busy — he is controlling the universe, he is redeeming people. He is doing so much. But his big effort is over. His big effort was creating the universe. When God had finished, he rested.

77

Notice that in Genesis there was no evening of the seventh day. He went on enjoying that rest.

Sunday, in a sense, is a little taste of rest for us because we do cease from our own labours as God did from his. But the phrase "cease from our own works" means something much deeper to us. God's Sabbath rest is to be enjoyed by human beings in this sense. God doesn't want me to be living in the power of my flesh but in the power of his Spirit. He doesn't want me to be trying to do what I think is right, he wants me to be enjoying doing what he says is right. He doesn't want me to be striving in my own strength to do things, he wants me to be enjoying his strength to do them.

Joshua got the people into the right place for rest but not into the right rest. When you attend a church service, whether you go out rested or exhausted, depends on you. To rest in God is to stop trying to do your own thing and rest in him. That was how you began the Christian life, wasn't it? You look back over the crises in your Christian life when you have really been going under, is it not because you have been trying to do things yourself? As soon as you stopped trying and let him take over, what happened? You were through. This will be how you will get to heaven as well. You don't have to struggle to get there. When you come to die you will rest in the Lord and he will carry you there.

That is the secret of resting. You can still do many things, but now you are not trying to do your own things, you are resting in him. Enter into the Sabbath rest of God!

So finally, we ask the very practical question *how* do I enter into the Sabbath rest? That I may not make the mistake those Hebrews made in the wilderness. The answer is very simple—through the Word of God. It is living and active, which is why it is often called a "seed". Plant it deep within your heart and it germinates and produces. It is like a two-edged sword, which was one of the two main weapons of

Roman soldiers. One was a long, thin sword more like the ones we are accustomed to seeing, and one was a short, fat sword shaped exactly like a tongue, an impression which was also conveyed by a strengthening line running down the middle. This was the two-edged sword, which a soldier used to slash with, and it could go clean through a man's bone. It was a deadly weapon. Here the Word of God is living, powerful and active, sharper than any two-edged sword, splitting the marrow from the bone and the spirit from the soul. The word "soul" there means, as it does in the Bible, simply physical life. (It is a word used of animals in Genesis 1. They were living souls.) "Spirit" here means spiritual, heavenly life. The Word of God can split between those two. The person wielding that sword has eyes, and nothing can be hidden from the God who speaks. There is a vivid word used here, *trachilos*, it comes from the same word as neck, *trachiatus*. It means to hold someone by the throat and force them to look into your eyes. It is a vivid term, boldly used of God. One day he will say, "Look into my face, look at me. Did you harden your heart when I spoke, or did you soften it?" We will struggle then to look away; we will want to look down. That is where you want to look when you are ashamed or embarrassed. But God will say: look at me; my Word was living and active but you ignored it; you grumbled and complained and you never entered my rest.

It has been said that it was comparatively easy for God to get Israel out of Egypt but it was very hard for God to get Egypt out of Israel. Do you understand that? Can I put it in Christian terms? It is comparatively easy to get a Christian out of the world; it is not so easy to get the world out of the Christian — which is holiness. For too long, Christians have thought that holiness and happiness therefore consisted of getting Christians out of the world. Believe me, that's not the secret. The secret is getting the world out of Christians.

All through the wilderness the root problem was that although Israel was out of Egypt, there was still too much Egypt in Israel. They kept looking back to it and they kept saying, "Why did you bring us out of Egypt? We used to eat garlic and onions and gravy and it was nice. Manna — horrible stuff," That is why they didn't get into the promised land. Christ not only rescues us out of something, he wants to redeem us into something. He not only wants us out of a land that is bad for us but into a land that is good for us. He not only wants us Christians, he wants us to be spiritual Christians enjoying the promises of God, going all the way until in the promised land we rest in him.

4

BETTER THAN HIGH PRIEST
Read 4:14 – 6:20

A. HIGH PRIESTHOODS (4:14–5:10)
1. Sympathises – tempted (4:14–16)
2. Sacrifices – appointed (5:1–6)
3. Suffers – perfected (5:7–10)
B. HAZY PRINCIPLES (5:11–6:8)
1. Arrested – infancy (5:11–14)
2. Advanced – maturity (6:1–3)
3. Abandoned – apostasy (6:4–8)
C. HOPEFUL PROMISES (6:9–20)
1. Earnestness – heir (6:9–12)
2. Encouragement – oath (6:13–18)
3. Entry – anchor (6:19–20)

Now we come to the fourth contrast: that Jesus is better than the high priest and all the priests of the Old Testament because he really succeeds in doing for us what those priests failed to do. Remember that the writer of Hebrews is addressing Jews who have professed to become Christians. He is trying to show them that they must leave their Jewish religion behind. They must leave behind their dependence on prophets, angels, priests, Moses and Joshua, and they must look only to Jesus. We need only Christ and to look only to him and we have everything we could wish for.

From Hebrews 4:14 onwards there are many connecting links with what has gone on before, and you notice that the writer has a habit of mentioning some three times the things he is going to talk about before he talks about them. Have you noticed that in this passage the name "Melchizedek" came three times? Yet not one word was said by way of explanation and you are left asking what all that was about. Who was he and why was he included? We will return to that later. In the same way, already Christ has been referred to as "priest" in the first four chapters, yet no word of explanation has been provided concerning why that title has been given to him.

Now we have reached the point where the writer will expand on what he has mentioned. As you read through the rest of the letter, look for these key ideas that he mentions without any explanation. Then you know that a big subject is coming up on the horizon; it is a kind of *hors d'oeuvre* and he is a very wise teacher because he gives tasty little appetizers to whet your appetite to learn more. In fact, he now says in this chapter, "I wish I could give you a whole plate full of meat right at the beginning, but you don't have the appetite." We are out of the shallows now and we are going very deep in the next few chapters. I hope you will stretch your mind, think hard and meditate upon these wonderful things.

We look first at the high priesthood of Christ. Now what is the task of a high priest? What's his job? Since we don't have them, we have got to think a bit about this and ask what he was there for. The answer is very simple. The high priest was there to get men and God together; it is as simple as that. He was a man who had to go to God as a representative of the people. He had to relate the people to God and he had to get them near to God. He was the vital link between God and man. They couldn't do without him because ordinary men could not approach God. They had to have a priest who would do this for them. You and I would have no right whatever to go direct to God. We have got to go through a priest; everybody has to because we are just not fit, as sinners,

to approach a holy God. To show us that sinners need to keep
their distance, God has taught us clearly that we must have
a priest who will be the intermediary, the go-between, the
link between men and God. If he is going to do this well, he
must know God very well and he must know men very well.
He must have an understanding of the divine nature and he
must have an understanding of human nature.

The problem with most priests is they are lacking in one
or the other. Neither understanding is perfect in any human
priest. Some human priests understand sinful nature only
too well because they share it; they don't understand the
divine nature so well. Other human priests have had such a
rarefied spiritual experience that though they understand God
well, they just seem to have got out of touch with people.
They seem to be way out of reach. But Jesus is the perfect
high priest because he was the Son of God and understood
God perfectly, and because he became the Son of Man and
understands human nature perfectly. That is why we don't
need any priest but one. We come to God through Jesus
Christ, our Lord. Every prayer we pray is prayed through
our priest, through Jesus Christ, the one who perfectly
understands God and the one who perfectly understands us.

The first part of our study of this passage concentrates on
the human side. How can the Son of God understand me?
How can this person — who lived in eternal glory right next
to God, who is God, who shared everything that God had,
who created the world with God — understand me? The
answer is threefold. First, he can *sympathise* because he
has been tempted. Second, he can *offer sacrifice* because
he has been appointed, and third, because he has *suffered*
he has been perfected as a priest. Now let us look at these
three thoughts.

Let me say straightaway that I do not believe that Jesus
has suffered every temptation I have, and I certainly have not

suffered every temptation he has. I have never been tempted to turn stones into bread. Have you? Now this just underlines that the temptations that came to him are different in form to the temptations that came to us. The phrase, "tempted at all points" means not that he has had every temptation, but that he has known the pressure of the devil at his most sensitive point as I have known the temptation of the devil at my most sensitive point. The phrase "at all points" is a technical phrase taken from a soldier's armour. However well made a suit of armour is, with all its plates riveted together, there are always some places that are weak. They have to be because the armour must move—under the arm is one place. There are certain places that, because they are jointed and move, are chinks in the armour. Therefore, if we translated this colloquially, it might be said that "he has been tempted at all chinks like as we are." The devil knows exactly how to get hold of you. He knows your weakest point; he knows your sensitive spot and that is where he makes for.

This is indeed a normal principle of warfare: you study your enemy, you see where he is strong, you see where he is weak, and you attack the weak point. If you study the temptations of Jesus, all three were at his most sensitive points. Not that they were our temptations, but that he has known what they are. Do you realise that he has suffered more temptations than any of us for a very simple reason? Because the devil can get us before he pulls the worst temptation out of the bag. We don't go right down the line saying "no" until he brings out the very last and worst temptation. We give in some way down the line. Do you realise that if you are sinless, you have got to suffer the whole line of temptation, right down to the very worst? So that Jesus has been tempted more than we are; we have given way at a certain point when our resistance has broken down. But he went down the whole way, to the very worst that the devil could throw at him. So you have to be sinless to feel the full force of temptation and it is because of this that he is sympathetic. Now it is an awful question: supposing Jesus had sinned and the devil had got him at the beginning of his ministry, what would have happened? One dreads to think, but he could not then have gone on to die for our sins. He could not have offered a perfect sacrifice to God. In fact, what could God have done? He had only one Son to send. Nobody could have been saved had that happened, but thank God it didn't happen so we need not pursue the speculation. But I believe the temptation could not have been real to Jesus if he could not sin. What is so real is his humanity — that temptation presented him with a real opportunity and a real possibility of doing wrong. Having felt the pressure, he is a high priest who understands.

Next time you are under pressure or feeling all the force of temptation, run to Jesus, because he understands. Hear him say: "I know just how you feel, but I didn't give way and I'll help you not to." That is how a high priest who really understands can talk. Therefore, we have v. 16, which is one of the most choice jewels in the whole New Testament: we can now come to the throne of grace with confidence.

If you were approaching a God you felt didn't understand, if you were approaching a God away up in heaven who had never been tempted, and who just was outside all these pressures, you might be tempted to say, "I'm not going to a God like that; he won't understand. He doesn't understand the pressure. He doesn't understand what it's like to fight the devil. He's all powerful, he can just snap his fingers and the devil's got to go." But you can't say that now — you can come with confidence.

You can ask for mercy for the past when you have fallen and you can ask for grace for the future that you might not fall again, because you are talking to someone who has been tempted. What a high priest to have! Don't you feel a little more confident when you are confessing to someone who has been tempted that much, who has known the battle, who understands human nature, but who won the battle, who is able to say, "I've felt all the pressure of it, but I came out on top and I can help you to do the same." Treasure 4:16. Underline that verse in your Bible and meditate on it.

Not only does Jesus sympathise, but he is able to offer sacrifice because that is the job of the priest too. If he is to get people through to God, he must offer a sacrifice for sin. He must make some compensation and it must be the compensation of blood, of life—an innocent life for a guilty one. All through the Old Testament they sacrificed the lives of innocent animals—little lambs without blemish. They would offer that as compensation to pay God back for the loss of the guilty life of the person who was trying to draw near. We will look more at this notion of sacrifice but if a priest is going to do this, then he must do it by divine appointment. Just as you see the royal crest and "By appointment" on certain trade signs, so every priest must have on him the crest "By divine appointment". Nobody dared offer a sacrifice to God unless God appointed them to do so. They have no authority, no right.

Let us look now at the first high priest, Aaron. There are three ways in which Aaron and Jesus are alike and three ways in which they are different, corresponding to the same three things. First of all, both were selected by God. Both received divine appointment, but here is the difference: Aaron was appointed as a servant; Jesus is the Son. There it is again. Second similarity and difference: both offered sacrifices for sins, but Aaron had to offer a sacrifice for his own sin before he could offer it for anyone else. Jesus never had to do that. When he died on the cross, he offered a sacrifice for everybody else's sin. The third difference is that Aaron was sympathetic with human nature *because he himself sinned*. That tends to make you unbalanced. It is a difficult thing to strike the balance in your attitude to sinners. There are two extremes. One is to be hard, indifferent and unsympathetic. The other is to say, "Well I've done that too," and be so sympathetic that you don't treat it really as sin. In other words, you can go to one of two extremes. You are either on the extreme of being apathetic toward sin or the extreme of being sentimental about it. A good high priest is someone who can sympathise yet still call it sin. Aaron had the problem that he had sinned himself, and therefore his sympathy tended to be towards the sentimental and to excuse another's sin as what he had done himself. But Jesus had all the sympathy yet none of the sins. Therefore, he could say to a woman taken in adultery, with tremendous sympathy, "Neither do I condemn you." What sympathy, but listen, "Go and sin no more." Do you see the difference? We tend to get this out of balance, tending to be over strict with sins we have not committed and under strict with sins we have, and that is a human weakness. Parents are the same way with children. Do you not tend to be a little more lenient to your own children's sins when those sins are the sins you commit? Of course, when you have children they inherit all your weaknesses, don't they? You see coming out in them the very things that you don't like in yourself. So it is very difficult to be balanced in your discipline towards the children. You would probably excuse the things you know that you are guilty of as well. To get the right balance between sympathy and sternness is very difficult. Jesus does; Aaron couldn't. You remember that Aaron, himself, made some awful mistakes including a golden calf, but Jesus didn't make any mistakes.

Thirdly, Jesus has been made a perfect high priest because he suffered and learned obedience. Now that doesn't mean that he started off in life as our children start off: disobedient. Children learn the word "no" before they learn the word "yes". Have you discovered that? We start with a disobedient, rebellious nature. That nature has to be trained to be obedient. Jesus didn't start that way, but what does "learned obedience" mean? It doesn't mean that he was disobedient before. Somebody has put it superbly: it is the difference between innocence and virtue, which are not the same thing.

Innocence is to do the right thing without knowing the wrong thing and without having been tested or tempted. Virtue is doing the right thing in face of temptation to do the wrong thing. Obedience in the boy Jesus was, I am sure, a natural attribute, but it became a virtue and not innocence when he faced the wrong thing and said no to it. There is a great difference between innocence and virtue. A baby doesn't have virtue, but it does have innocence. You see the difference? So you look at a baby and think, "What an innocent little child. How many sins they're not committing! They are not gossiping about other people; they are not committing all the sins that we find in the adult world. What a lovely, innocent baby. I wish I was innocent like that."

But there is something greater than being innocent and that is being virtuous — having come to the point where you know the alternative and still say no to it. In a sense, many children in Christian homes have an artificial innocence, which is not necessarily virtue or righteousness. It is just that they have not been exposed to the alternative. A child from a Christian home really finds out if their faith is real when they get away from home and out into a world that is totally different from a Christian environment and then say no to the alternative. Then innocence becomes virtue. In Jesus' innocence, he was born in innocence, but he became virtuous. He learned obedience—he had done it naturally until he learned the alternative and then he did it voluntarily. He learned obedience by the things he suffered and how he suffered.

Time and again you see Jesus in agony. Believe me, temptation could bring drops of blood to his brow. I guess you've never been tempted so much that drops of blood appeared on your forehead through the pores, but his sweat became as drops of blood. It is a condition that a doctor once told me is possible. He went through agony and strong cries and tears, says the scripture. He didn't learn obedience the easy way; he learned it the very hardest way, a harder way than we ever have to learn it because he suffered worse temptations. For this reason, he became the perfect high priest because he was an obedient high priest – a sinless high priest, having been through it all, he came out triumphant.

So much for the high priesthood as compared with Aaron. So we have the greatest high priest – "Since we have a great high priest..." and he is not on earth. We don't need him on earth, we need him where it matters—where God is. So he has gone into the heavens as our great high priest and there he prays for us.

At this point, the author of this letter realises he is getting deeper and deeper, and he is just pausing for a moment and thinking of those who are going to read and listen. Perhaps he is wondering how many are switching off. I am afraid he guesses that quite a few may be, because he recognises that what he is giving is not milk but meat. Milk takes very little taking in doesn't it? I drink a lot of milk — having learned the habit on the farm I have never got rid of it. It is no bother. You can get a whole lot of nourishing food and you don't have to chew it — just a single swallow and it's down. Great! But meat is a different matter. You are supposed to chew each mouthful fifty times if you are going to get the most out of it and digest it properly! The trouble is that when we come to church, when we listen to God's Word, we can want milk; just a good swallow and it's over—no effort. But the author here says, "I want to give you meat. I want you to chew it over; take it home and chew it over at home. Read it through again." Frankly, this is the only way that I can prepare a sermon: I read the passage through and I don't get much out of it, so I read it a second time and I get a little out of it then. Then I read it a third time and a little more comes; then I read it a fourth time and more comes. I just chew and chew and chew. I believe that anybody who is willing to chew the Bible will be able to digest it and get some real nourishment. But the tragedy is that physically and spiritually it is possible to have arrested growth—tragic when it happens physically, as when a child fails to grow up, fails to develop mentally or physically, but it is even more tragic when it happens spiritually. It is due to one thing: mental laziness, unwillingness to think for yourself, becoming intellectually sluggish. Getting the truth out of God's Word is not a matter of your IQ – thank God it isn't.

Whatever your IQ, if you are lazy in spiritual things, then you won't get nourishment from God's Word. You cannot read the Bible as you read your newspaper—just the headlines and a few paragraphs and it's finished for the day. Arrested development is due to becoming spiritually deaf, dull of hearing, people who haven't grown up as Christians, who are still in the primary, in the kindergarten.

Do you know it positively hurts me if somebody who has been a Christian for twenty or thirty years tells me they prefer children's addresses to sermons? It is a remark that goes through me like a knife. It breaks my heart to think that somebody who has been walking with the Lord for so long still finds it easier to go to a family service and listen to a children's talk —that is tragic, it really is. Still wanting dollops of milk. "But let's not do that," says Hebrews. Such arrested development will have a profound effect on your moral judgment. Much moral misjudgment is due to mental laziness. You see, some people want the Bible to be a book of answers to every moral question so that they can look up the text and there is the answer. The Bible is not that kind of a book. Time and again, one is confronted with moral decisions through life that are not dealt with directly in the Bible. How do we settle them? The answer is very simple: if you have used your mind and matured and developed, then, says this author, you will instinctively be able to distinguish right from wrong. You will have a mature outlook on moral questions because you have thought them through and used your mind and you are steeped in God's outlook and you have the mind that was in Christ, so you are able to distinguish good from evil.

Mental laziness will produce moral perplexity. You will be running around for advice and guidance to all kinds of people because you cannot distinguish for yourself. You have not grown up enough to know instinctively, when a course of action is before you, that is right or wrong. Whereas mental maturity produces moral insight and you become not so much clever as wise. You are able, then, to give advice to others.

You ought to be teaching other people now, not listening to someone yourself. You ought to be teachers. By now, from all you have heard, you ought to be passing it on.

Let us then advance and go on; there is need for progress. In 6:1–2 the author lists the kind of kindergarten ABC, the things that you ought to need no teaching about whatever: repentance, faith, baptism, the laying on of hands, resurrection and judgment. Those are six fundamentals which every new Christian ought to have mastered. We ought not to need to preach on them to Christians. We should be able to build on that foundation and go on. That is an interesting list. The first two relate us to God, the second two relate us to the church, and the last two relate us to the future. We ought to have a clear foundation in our mind concerning these truths.

In 6:4–6 we come to perhaps the most controversial passage in the whole of the New Testament. This language is very strong: "Those who have once been enlightened, who have tasted the heavenly gift, who have shared in the Holy Spirit, who have tasted the goodness of the Word of God and the powers of the coming age...." That language is of one who has gone a long way into Christianity. What is meant is turning one's back on Christ and saying, "I deny Christ; I disavow Christ; I turn right away from him." Of the person who does that, this passage is saying, "There is no hope for that man." You will never get him back to repentance. Now a backslider can get back, but an apostate never can. Why? Because he has cut off his only line of retreat. He has cut off the cross; he has put Christ back on the cross. He has lined up with those who rejected Christ. He is exposing Christ to public shame and humiliation. He is turning his back on Christ; he can never get back.

The danger is that if we do not go on to maturity, we can find ourselves drifting to the point where we actually commit apostasy. That is the message here, and I take it in its context. It is the whole drift, if you will forgive the pun, of the letter to the Hebrews. How shall we escape if we neglect, if we drift away? Don't drift away; get an anchor down. Don't drift on to the rocks of apostasy. Don't wake up one morning and realise that you have, in fact, turned your back on Christ and that you cannot get back again. We must take the warning seriously.

A good Bible study is to look up the four impossible things in the letter to the Hebrews. This is the first: that a man who turns his back on Christ and denies his own experience of the Holy Spirit, finishes himself. There is no hope of getting back; he is absolutely lost. I believe we cannot get around the meaning of the words.

But the writer of the letter to the Hebrews doesn't want readers to despair and to go home neurotically depressed. "Have I committed this or have I not? Am I an apostate or am I not?" for backsliders often think they are. If you want to prove whether you are a backslider or an apostate, there is a very simple test: go back to Christ and see if he will have you. If you are a backslider, he will have you straight back; if you are an apostate, you can't. So apply that test. Just go to Christ for forgiveness. If you are a backslider, he will welcome you back with open arms, but that doesn't deny the warning.

The writer to the Hebrews, describing the possibility, not as something merely hypothetical but as a real possibility, does not say, "If *you* fall away" but, "If *they* fall away." It keeps it impersonal. He wants them to take warning. Now he goes back to "you" and says, "But I'm persuaded of better things of you. Already you've shown your love for the church; you've shown your love for your fellow Christians. Already you've expressed your faith in works. God will not forget this. I'm persuaded that you won't do this. Oh, I'm confident that you're going to respond to my appeal and you're not going to drift back to that. You're going to go on ... stop drifting. You need an anchor."

Then there is a call to imitate the great men of faith who have persevered. Now if somebody says to me, "Do you believe in the perseverance of the saints?" I say, "Yes, I most certainly do. They do need to persevere." You persevere by getting that anchor ahead of you and pulling on it.

To stop a ship drifting with the tide, you have got to have an anchor down. The anchor will be invisible, but the ship will hold. In the drift and the tide of human affairs; in the drift of society, in the tide of fashion, a Christian will just be swept along unless he has got an anchor and is holding on. The only thing that holds a man still when society is moving past him is an anchor. What is that anchor? Let us go way back to Abraham, for that is where the letter to the Hebrews starts. Abraham was a saint who persevered. He hung on until the promises came true. He didn't drift back. He never went back to Ur of the Chaldees. What did Abraham hang on to? He hung on to what you can hang on to: that God cannot lie. When God says something, he can't lie and when he wants to emphasise that he is not lying, he swears. When he promised to Abraham that he would multiply and bless him with descendants, God not only said, "I'll do this," he said, "I swear by myself I'll do it." When God says a thing and then swears it, you have two immutable things to hang on to. You are absolutely sure; you have got every reason for confidence. God cannot lie. Therefore you hang on to that word.

But we have something even better than a promise made to Abraham. We have Jesus and he is the Word. In him all the promises of God find their "Yes" and "Amen". So we have even greater proof that God cannot lie. That is your anchor and it is invisible — every anchor is when it is doing its job. Our anchor is within the veil, beyond sight — it is in the heavens, but that is what I am holding on to. It is what you should be holding on to. That is what gives you the strength of conviction to think, "He is able to keep that which I've committed...." You don't find people talking like that unless they are hanging on to the anchor, do you? They are filled with doubts and uncertainties when they let go of the anchor and they drift. So we finish up with the ground of the Christian security. Imitate Abraham's faith. Since we have an anchor within the veil, hang on to the anchor and there will be no danger of apostasy in your life.

There is a solemn warning here. At the end of chapter 6, the anchor and the high priest link up. Have you noticed that? The anchor is a person; the anchor is a high priest. If you have Jesus there pleading with the Father for you, hang on to Jesus; he hangs on to you. This is your anchor; this is your security; this is your stability, Not that you were converted twenty years ago, but that you are hanging on to Jesus now.

5

BETTER THAN AARON
Read 7:1 – 28

A. FIRST PATTERN (7:1–10)
1. Immortal priest – Melchizedek (1–3)
      a. His description (1)
      b. His denomination (2)
      c. His duration (3)
2. Inferior patriarch (4–10)
      a. What he gave (4–6a, 8–10)
      b. What he got (6b–7)
B. FINAL PERFECTION (11–28)
1. Imperfect law – Aaron (11–19)
      a. Not by lineage (11–14)
      b. But by life (15–19)
2. Indestructible life – Jesus (20–28)
      a. Oath (20–22)
      b. Office (23–25)
      c. Offering (26–28)

Wth Hebrews chapter seven, we come to a very characteristic thought of this letter, but one which sits strangely in Protestant thinking. Paradoxically, denominations which call their ministers "priests" understand the central part of the letter to the Hebrews better. But if they understood it better still, then they should not have any priests! There is a dilemma. Those churches that don't have priests and are not used to having them find this all a little strange, talking about Aaron and Melchizedek and what the priest's job was.

But understand that if it were not for Jesus Christ, you would need to have a priest. Indeed, if you are a believer it is true to say that you do have the best priest of all. If you did not have such a great high priest, you would not be able to contact God. You would not be able to have communion with him. You would not know him. You would call on him from a distance but never feel that intimacy which you now feel.

The Latin word for "priest" is *pontifex*, from which we get all kinds of other words like pontificate, and it means simply "a bridge builder". That is what a priest's job is. He is the bridge builder to cross the very big gulf between men and God. It is not only due to the fact that we are creatures, and he is the Creator. Nor is it only that we are on earth and he is in heaven. It is primarily due to the fact that we are sinful and he is holy, and that is the biggest gap of all, which none of us can cross. It requires a priest to be a *pontifex*, a bridge builder between man and God.

There is only one such for us, and he is Jesus Christ, the perfect high priest, and all other priests fade into insignificance by comparison with Jesus. Once we have him, we need no other. That is the glorious gospel and why you never hear me called a priest. We need pastors but not priests. Indeed, *you* are a priest. We believe in the priesthood of all believers, but there is one great high priest — Jesus Christ.

To develop this theme, the author of this letter is going back into the Old Testament. Remember that he is writing for Jewish Christians, and that is why this letter is a little strange to some of us Gentile believers. We ought to be able to say everything we need to say about Jesus Christ from the Old Testament. After all, the early church had to as they had no New Testament. They were too busy living it, and then, a few decades later, they were writing it.

At 7:1–10 we go back to "the first pattern of priesthood"

in the Bible, which is, surprisingly, not the Jewish priesthood but a Gentile priesthood. If you want to find out the original pattern of priesthood in God's mind, you have got to go way back beyond Aaron, beyond Levi, beyond Moses — back beyond Abraham. You have to go back to the point where God's first priest is mentioned, and he is not a Jew — that is very significant. The first priest of the most high God is God's pattern for priesthood. The later priests of the Old Testament were all Jewish and only ministered to Jews. There were only Jewish high priests. The original pattern is what we go back to. This is a principle that runs right through scripture. If you want God's original pattern of marriage, you must go back beyond the divorce laws of Moses to the original pattern in Genesis 2. That is what Jesus did when he was asked about Moses' divorce laws. Jesus took us back to the original pattern of marriage, family life and so much else, and in priesthood he took us back to the original. The original is a man called Melchizedek. We have already encountered him three times in the letter to the Hebrews. You must have kept wondering, "What on earth does that name keep cropping up for?"

Melchizedek is only mentioned twice in the Old Testament, once in Psalm 110 about a thousand years before Christ, and once nearly two thousand years before Christ. It is in Genesis 14:14ff. When Abraham learned that Lot had been captured, he called together the men born into his household, 318 of them in all, and chased after the retiring army as far as Dan. That night he successfully attacked them and pursued the fleeing army to north of Damascus, and recovered everything: the loot that had been taken, his relative Lot, and all of Lot's possessions, the women and other captives. As Abram returned from his strike against Chedorlaomer and the other kings at the valley of Shaveh, later called King's Valley, the king of Sodom came out to meet him and Melchizedek, the king of Salem or Jerusalem, who was a priest of the God of highest heaven, brought him bread and wine. Then Melchizedek blessed Abram with this blessing: the blessing of the supreme God, Creator of heaven and earth, be upon you Abram, and blessed be God who has delivered your enemies over to you. Then Abram gave Melchizedek a tenth of all the spoils.

Let us look at the significance of this. A strange figure, long before Abraham became the father of believers, the founder of the nation Israel, the friend of God, and long before God called Abraham out of Ur of the Chaldees, God was truly worshipped. One of the most fascinating things revealed by the study of the history of religion is that religion did not begin with the worship of idols and lots of gods and demons. Religion, the earlier we go back, the purer it becomes until when you get back to the first trace of religion in the human race it is the worship of one God most high above the sky, who made the earth. All the introduction of animism and spiritism and worship of idols and images has come in later. So in the beginning, religion was pure and men worshipped the God most high. Redemption was needed because men fell from their original knowledge of God.

Long before Abraham settled in the promised land, Jerusalem was already a holy city. Long before a single Jew lived in it there was a priest in it, and the priest was the king of it. This is the only time in the entire Old Testament when a man fulfils both functions of king and priest. Never in the entire course of Jewish history was one man up to holding both jobs. God had to keep them separate because no man was big enough to do both jobs. So he said, "The tribe of Levi shall be the priests, and the tribe of Judah shall be the kings" —but never the same people. Yet here in the beginning is the holy city of Jerusalem, called already "Jerusalem". "Jeru" means "city" or "foundation" and "salem" "shalom, peace."

Already there is a city of peace reigned over by a king who is the priest, and who not only leads his people politically but spiritually.

A nation needs a leader like this, and Melchizedek led his people and that was a holy city long before Abraham got there, long before King David captured it and made it the capital of Israel. So it is the holy city not first for Jews but for everybody. That is what God intends it to be at the end of history, and that is what it will be. That's what the New Jerusalem will be — a city for Gentile and Jew to worship the most high God.

Now look at three things about Melchizedek, the Gentile king and priest: his *description*, his *denomination*, and his *duration*. First, his description: king and priest. The phrase "God most high" was used even by the ancient Phoenicians, the people who first discovered how to navigate by the stars and who in those days used to get in their boats and come to Cornwall for tin. Wherever you go in the world if you trace back man's spiritual pilgrimage far enough, you come back to the God most high. This is the God we worship now. There is only one God; he is the God most high, the God supreme, Creator of heaven and earth. King and priest, sovereign.

Now look at the *denomination* or the *names* which he is given because names are very important in scripture. They are not just favourite names or names to give someone a unique personality, they are names to describe God's plan and God's nature for them. So he had, first of all, the name Melchizedek — "melchi" means "king" and "zedek" means "righteousness". What a name for a king — King Righteousness! Therefore, his city was called Jerusalem, foundation of peace, shalom.

Notice the order of the two names. The reason why we cannot call our towns cities of peace is that we don't have kings of righteousness. Until you have the righteousness, you can't have the peace. Righteousness and peace kiss each other, and this is the order. When Jesus was born: glory to God in the highest and peace on earth. We have been trying to get peace on earth without glory to God in the highest ever since, and failing. So the real order is: king of righteousness, city of peace, and if you have the King of Righteousness reigning in your heart then your heart becomes a citadel of peace, and the two are related. So these are his very significant names.

The next thing here is something that the Bible doesn't say. It is just as important to notice what the Bible doesn't say as what it does say. If you realise that, you will get even more out of your Bible. A good reference is good because of what it says and what it doesn't say. Now Melchizedek has a written reference from God here. There are certain things said about him: he was a king of righteousness, he ruled over a city of peace. Many things are said about him, but there are certain things missing from the reference, and these are just as significant as the things that are given. There is no reference to his mother and father. There is no reference to any children. There is no reference to the date of his birth, and there is no reference to the date of his death, and these are highly significant. Why? Because what God says is important, and what he doesn't say is important, and that is how we are to read our Bibles.

The writer of Hebrews knew how to read his Bible, and he read this and he said, "It doesn't mention father or mother, no date of birth, no date of death, no succession of priesthood—that is terribly important to a priest." Every later priest had to prove his birth, his descendants, his father and mother, and it is recorded. Read through the first few chapters of the book of Chronicles — many "begats" were to prove priesthood. Yet Melchizedek stands alone and appears neither to begin nor to end. God gives only two priests of this order. Of the Levitical order, of the Aaronic order there were hundreds. There were in fact thirty-two high priests from the beginning of the days of the priesthood — Moses and Aaron — through to the fall of the temple. There were hundreds of priests attending the high priests. But Melchizedek stands alone, and there is only one more belonging to his order of priesthood in the whole of scripture: Jesus. They are like each other insofar as they do not depend for their priesthood on their father and mother. They do not depend on their birth. They do not cease to be priests at their death. They have this quality of an immortal priesthood.

Melchizedek is still a priest of God most high. All other priests have ceased to be priests; they died, and the succession passed on down the line. But not Melchizedek, he is a priest forever. So God says to his son Jesus, "You are a priest forever in the order of Melchizedek." This is the kind of priest you need. Jesus has neither beginning nor end of days but is the eternal high priest. That's how he can meet your need now.

We now see the relationship between Melchizedek and Abram, as he was then called. The Jews held Abraham in the highest respect; he was the father of the nation. But now the letter argues that Abraham was not the greatest because Melchizedek blessed Abraham, and the greater blesses the lesser. What a brilliant argument from Abraham's own life to a Jew who tends not to give to Melchizedek the place he deserves. In fact, consider first of all the things that Abraham gave to Melchizedek and then consider the things that Melchizedek gave to Abram. They are profoundly significant. Abraham gave Melchizedek a tenth of all that he had won in battle because Melchizedek was greater. Now look at what Melchizedek gave Abram. He gave him his blessing, and you can't bless someone else unless you have more blessing than they have, and give them from your greater blessing. You can't bless someone unless you have a blessing to give and Melchizedek blessed Abram.

More than that, and Christians can't help feeling the significance of this, this king-priest of Jerusalem brought Abram bread and wine. So that's our Jesus and Melchizedek doing the same thing. Though Abraham was a very great man, consider this, says the letter, consider; turn it over in your mind — even Abraham was secondary to Melchizedek.

Now we move on in the argument. From the original pattern, the first pattern of priesthood, to the final perfection of priesthood — and the jump is immediate because there is nothing in between. In this priesthood, there was only the first pattern and the final perfection, only the two examples. Because there are only the two examples, everything else in between is now obsolete and vanishes from our view. All the high priests and priests in between vanish, and our thinking jumps straight from Melchizedek to Jesus. This is where our thinking is going to go now.

It could have been argued that because Aaron and the Levites came later than Melchizedek that they were greater; that they replaced the earlier. I am afraid that is our thinking. We always think that the latest is the best, don't we? That something new is better than something old is not true. Because Aaron and the Levites came after Melchizedek, I am afraid Jews tended to think of them as more important — but not with God. King David himself, the king of Israel, sang, "The Lord said to my Lord, sit at my right hand," and "I have sworn forever you are a priest according to the order of Melchizedek. When I swear, I will not change my mind." There in King David, a thousand years after Melchizedek, right in the mid point, in the gap, David looks back and forwards, back to Melchizedek and to one more Lord who is going to come and be a priest of the same kind. Isn't the pattern of God's revelation remarkable? Two thousand years' gap and right in the middle this mention again of Melchizedek to link the two and keep them reminded of the original pattern of priesthood.

So, therefore, vv. 11–19 tell us quite clearly that the system of priesthood under Aaron and under the law of Moses was less than the best. It was imperfect. In fact, it failed. It is quite obvious that it was not good enough because God changed the system. The system was that you had to be born in the tribe of Levi, so God changed the system and got a Melchizedek priest from the tribe of Judah. That tribe is never mentioned as producing priests in the Old Testament. In fact, God not only changed the tribe but he wasn't bothered about tribe at all — because Jesus wasn't a priest because he was born of Judah but because he had the quality in himself of an everlasting life, and that is what was needed.

Let us look at why the old law and the old priesthood failed. I'll tell you why: the bridge never got built. In the lovely city of Brasilia, which I visited many years ago, there was an oxbow lake, artificially created. There was only one sad thing that I saw there — an unfinished bridge. It would have been magnificent, with a great sweeping arch. There were just two ends sticking out from the banks of the lake, and there it had lain for years. It was about the only really unfinished thing in that beautiful city. This is precisely how we see the Old Testament priesthood. They tried to build the bridge between men and God, but they never got it built. The result was that men were never able to cross it, and they always had to keep their distance. Even though the priests offered sacrifices and prayed to God, and did all the necessary things, the people had to keep their distance. They couldn't even go into a holy place on earth, never mind think of going to heaven. So they kept away. The priests failed in that; they just never got them through.

There were other reasons for the priests' failure. One was

that the priest was the wrong side of the bridge to start with. He not only had to offer sacrifices for the sins of the people but for his own as well. Since none of them really worked, he had go on offering them every day, day after day. So the whole system was weak and useless. Strong language about the finest religion in the world before Christianity, but this is the language used.

This is the trouble. Religion never builds the bridge; only Christ is the *pontifex*. That is why religion doesn't get people through to God. They may say their prayers, they may go to church, but don't have that intimacy, that confidence, that holy boldness to call God "Abba, Father". You can see what people are trying to do, but the bridge never gets built. The people stay away from God and there is this sense of "God is remote."

Two men stood on the bridge of a ship one night in the middle of the Atlantic, there was a calm sea, the moon floated through the clouds, the stars were twinkling. One man who was a believer said to the captain of the ship, "It's easy to believe in God on a night like this, isn't it?" The captain said, "Yes, it is. A God who's as far away as those stars and as cold as that sea." Both believed in God, but one had a bridge and one didn't. This is what religion does for you. It may make you look towards God, look over the gulf. It may make you try and build a little bridge on your side and you try to build it by doing good and by not doing any harm and by going to church and by — whatever. But the bridge never gets across, does it? You never get the sense of, "I know God, he's with me. I love him and he loves me."

The whole Old Testament priesthood seemed to keep people at a distance. But when Jesus came, that whole system was obsolete because he was the bridge builder. "We have a better hope," says the writer, "because we can now come near to God." We can cross the bridge. We can come to God and say, "Abba, Father," through Jesus Christ our Lord.

So we come to the final part of the chapter. Jesus is our priest because of his indestructible life. Of all the priests in the Bible, Jesus was to be the best. Of the two priests of this special order of Melchizedek, Jesus was to be the perfect one. Even Melchizedek himself was not perfect. There are three ways in which Jesus has the perfect priesthood: *the oath of his priesthood; the office of his priesthood; the offering of his priesthood.*

Some people today take oaths before assuming an office — the more important the office, the more solemn the setting apart. The fact is that none of the Old Testament priests were ever sworn into office, but when Jesus became a priest, he was sworn in, for God has given us Jesus as a priest forever. No priest other than Jesus is ever sworn in for eternal life.

The second reason why Jesus is so much better even than Melchizedek is the office he holds. The contrast is between many priests and one. In the Old Testament, many priests died and were buried down the centuries, but when Jesus came he was the only one.

Now comes the most profound and yet the most practical sentence in this chapter, "Therefore, he is able to save to the uttermost...." This is often seriously misunderstood. I have heard it expounded as though it said, "He is able to save from the guttermost." Have you heard it interpreted in that way? That is not what it means. If I put it into literal, paraphrased English it might convey the meaning: "Therefore he is able to save for all time to the uttermost reaches of your existence." Why is he able to go on saving us? Because he will never have to stop praying for you. When Jesus prays he gets answers, and he ever lives to intercede for us. When he was on earth, he interceded for his own disciples. He said, "Peter, I've prayed for you. Watch that Satan should not get you." When Satan is troubling you, just remind yourself: "Christ is praying that Satan will not get me." Remember who is the stronger. Jesus is going to win that battle of prayer.

We don't to need comment much on the last three verses of the chapter because they are going to be expanded later. Every priest, if he is going to build a bridge to God, must offer a sacrifice of a life killed, with bloodshed to atone for the sinful life of the one who is trying to get near to God, to offer some compensation to God for a life that has been wasted. We don't have priests and we don't have altars because we don't need sacrifices. We only have a table to remember a sacrifice, we don't have an altar and a priest to offer one—a very important distinction. But the offering that this high priest made was the first time ever a priest offered himself, and the priest and the victim were one and the same. The reason why that could never have been done before, and Aaron, Levi and all the Levitical priests couldn't do it, was simply that none of them could offer a life in themselves that was pure, holy, blameless and separated from sinners. But all these qualifications are here listed. Jesus is holy in God's sight, blameless, unstained, separated from sinners, exalted in heaven. *He has got everything, not just to offer sacrifice but every qualification to be that sacrifice.*

If you had gone through the Jewish priesthood it would hit you forcefully that for the first time a priest did not bring a goat, bull, lamb or even a turtle dove; for the first time he just brought himself. He offered his own life and shed his own blood and offered the best and most acceptable sacrifice. "Behold the Lamb of God who takes away the sin of the world."

6

BETTER COVENANT
Read 8:1 – 9:22

A. MINISTER OF BETTER COVENANT (8:1–13)
1. Premises – space (1–5)
    a. Heavenly (1–3)
    b. Earthly (4–5)
2. Promises – time (6–13)
    a. Old (6–9)
    b. New (10–13)
B. MEDIATOR OF BLOOD COVENANT (9:1–22)
1. Premises – flesh (1:1–10)
    a. Visible (1–5)
    b. Invisible (6–10)
2. Promises – Spirit (11–22)
    a. Living (11–14)
    b. Dying (15–22)

I have the kind of mind that keeps asking "Why?" I want to know what the point of something is. I find it very difficult temperamentally to do a thing just because it is always done. There are many people who would say, "What is the point of coming to church? What's the point of spending so much time studying the Bible?" Particularly, the letter to the Hebrews, which delves into things with which many of us are totally unfamiliar, such as Old Testament ritual and ceremonies, Why do it? We are not in the Old Testament days, most of us are not even Jews.

At Hebrews 8:1 we see that we do have such a High Priest. In other words, we have got what the Jews had, only better. Is it better to have contact with the servant of a man or with his son? Which will give you more access to his heart and mind: to know the servant well or to know the son well? There is just no difficulty with the answer to that one. We have a much better religion than you can find anywhere else in the world. In fact, we have the best. Let's not be falsely modest about it. It is not just better, it's *best* because Christ could never be bettered.

There is a word that is coming in now — "covenant", which in fact occurs thirteen times in this passage. I want in particular to make a very strong distinction between the word "covenant" and the word "contract." Both are agreements between two parties but there is a profound difference between the two, and our agreement with God is never a contract. We are constantly trying to make it a contract but we can never do so. Jacob tried to make a contract with God the first night after he ran away from home. Being a mother's boy he was feeling very lonely, and he was looking forward to getting back again some day and he said, "God, if you'll bring me safely back home then I will do this, this, and this for you," and those were the terms of the contract. "Now, here you are Lord. You can sign here and then I'll sign there." That was Jacob's approach. On his way back home some years later God took him and so broke him that he limped — literally, he limped forever afterwards. God made a covenant with Jacob who then became "Israel", the father of the nation.

The trouble is that by nature we want a contract with God. "God, if I do this, will you do that? If I go to church once, or even maybe twice on Sunday, and that's pushing it, if I do this, that, and the other, if I'm kind to my neighbours, and if I don't do anybody any harm, then will you keep me

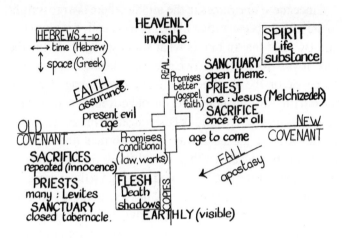

free from disease and bring me to a happy old age and open heaven up to me at the end?" Now that would be a contract like a life insurance policy, and that you cannot have with God. God doesn't make contracts, he makes covenants. (See my book *By God, I Will* for further discussion of the crucial distinction being made here and teaching on the biblical covenants.)

A biblical covenant is an agreement in which one of the two parties dictates the terms on his own will entirely and says, "These are the terms." The only thing the other party can do is accept or reject them. It is a one-sided, unilateral agreement. Wherever God enters into an agreement with man, he does it on the basis not of a contract but of a covenant. There is no room for bargaining.

So we have a covenant with God and Christ is the minister of a better covenant.

The diagram above is very simple. There is a line going across the middle and going straight up and down the middle. The line that goes along is a line representing time, and the line that goes up and down represents space.

Since these lines cross in the middle, there is a cross right in the middle because that in fact is what split time into AD and BC, and that in fact is what splits space also. It is the link, if you like, between two ages in time and two places in space. So on the timeline running across the page we have the old time and the new time, the old covenant and the new covenant, and the cross marks the transition in time from one to the other. In the same way, on the vertical line we have below the middle the earthly — and above the heavenly. So we have split time and space, and once again the cross is the meeting point between earth and heaven, and the two arms of the cross represent the two joinings of time and space.

Both of these systems were based on the promises of God. So I have written promises in the bottom left hand quarter and the top right hand quarter. In the old, earthly situation the promises were conditional; in the new situation the promises are much better. They belong to a whole new era. Notice: not only a new era in time but a new era in space. So if you are the right side of the cross you are not only in a new period of time, a new era, but you are in a new position, too. You are in the heavenlies rather than in the earthlies. In other words, a Christian has moved diagonally from the bottom left hand side to the top right hand. He has not only moved along, he has moved up.

The Jews used to call the old period "the present evil age". They looked for the "age to come" as a sort of golden era—the kingdom of God to come. The fact is that Christians are *already* living in the age to come. The new order has dawned; it is already here.

Likewise, if we take the vertical line, the earthly things were all copies. Everything the Jews had to help them in their worship were simply copies, models, imitations. The true things of which the earthlies were copies were in the heavenly realm. This applied to sacrifices, to priests, even to buildings and their shape. Are you beginning to get the pattern? So by faith we can move from the bottom left to the top right, and this will give us an assurance that we never had before—a boldness to approach God.

When considering Hebrews 6, we looked at the possibility of the reverse movement — falling through what we call "apostasy". So in the top left hand part of the page I have a diagonal arrow going up to the northeast—the arrow of faith. In the bottom right hand part of the paper, an arrow goes in a southwesterly direction and I have labelled it "fall and apostasy".

Now we can fill in a few more things. Let's go back to the bottom left hand corner. There are the words "sanctuary", "priests" and "sacrifices." They had all of these. They had a sanctuary which was a tabernacle which was kept closed; they had priests, many were Levites, and stemmed from Aaron; they had sacrifices which were repeated many times, sacrifices of innocent victims: lambs, bulls, and goats who had never sinned in their lives.

Now if we go up to the top right hand corner we write "sanctuary" again, but this time instead of closed it is open, and this time instead of a tent it is a throne. Then we write "priests" — this time instead of many priests we write one. Instead of the name of Aaron we write the name: "Melchizedek". We write sacrifices and this time we write not "innocence" but "obedience". For the first time a sacrifice was offered that was not based on innocence but obedience, and obedience is a far better thing than innocence. As I have said, a baby may be innocent but not obedient. The real virtue emerges not because of innocence, but because having faced temptation we have decided to be obedient. That was the sacrifice that Christ offered, which was better.

The result of all this, if we can sum it up, the bottom left hand corner we can sum up under the word "flesh", which with a little arrow leads to death, and the top right hand we can sum up in the word "spirit" which, with a little arrow, points to life. That is the difference, here you have the whole message of Hebrews. You can see just by the position on the diagram that the top right hand corner is better than the bottom left in almost every single particular.

The first thing that strikes me in 8:1 is that there is a combination of majesty and ministry. Here is someone sitting on a throne who serves—now that is a wonderful combination and it is just perfect.

Recall the foot washing when Peter said, "No you're not washing my feet, I'm not taking part in that." Peter was offended because the Lord was wanting to serve. But this is the High Priest we have and he is a perfect High Priest who didn't seek the position in order to lord it over others, far from it. He sought that position to serve. This was the difference between, on one hand, the two high priests who put Jesus to death — Annas and Caiaphas, who were both in it for the job, the money and the power, and on the other hand, the great High Priest we have who was in it to serve. So we have his majesty in heaven serving in the sanctuary. What a beautiful combination of majesty and ministry.

From that we go into two very simple things. Forgive the alliteration here but it seems to fit very well. We have a better religion because we have better *premises* and better *promises* and the two things are both mentioned here. Promises are mentioned actually by that word and the premises certainly are. They are just as important in God's thinking. We are to sit on the premises and stand on the promises, and they are both right here. But the tragedy is that Christian people today often mistake the premises we are supposed to have and think that we need an earthly sanctuary.

If you study church architecture the saddest thing about

so much of it is that it is trying to get an earthly sanctuary and it doesn't need it. It is trying to make a churchy looking building, something that is monumental rather than functional. This is a tragedy because it misses the whole point of the letter to the Hebrews. A church building on earth has no other function but to serve the needs of God's people, and to do that as efficiently as possible. It is not a monument and it is not there to be a sanctuary, for the very word implies something that is contrary to the New Testament.

Consider the premises. There are two sorts of premises: one built on earth and one built in heaven. Both Father and Son in the godhead are constructors. Anyone in the construction business should draw great inspiration from this. Jesus, the Son of God, was a carpenter and his Father was a builder and architect. So the Father built in heaven and ordered others to build on earth.

Imagine the tabernacle. Very simply it was a kind of box, which stood in the middle of the desert with a most gorgeously embroidered veil at one end, and inside it was divided into two square rooms. Around the box there was a curtain—in front there was an altar and in front of that a big bowl for washing. Smoke arose from the altar. The tents of the people of Israel were around—with certain tribes on particular sides. This, then, was the tabernacle of God on earth.

It was not worked out by Moses in any detail. They had no architect on earth, no designer. Moses was told to make this simply by being shown the original, for this was a copy; it was just a little thing. It is a copy of something that has never been built anywhere else on earth. It is a copy of something that exists in heaven. Moses was shown the pattern of heaven and God's home, and it was said: "Now, make a scaled down copy of that, put it on earth. Get down the details of everything you see." God gave him the way of translating it into earthly materials and how to do it. It was a most beautiful, in proportion, simple construction.

But the important thing is this: that this being only a copy is just slightly unreal. In fact, to give it that notion of being unreal, the word used is "shadow" — "it is only a shadow". A shadow is exactly the same shape as the real thing, or perhaps slightly distorted by the angle of light. But you can often tell who is passing a glass door by the shadow on it, can't you? You have a shadow which is different from my shadow. My shadow, in a sense, is part of me, yet I can live without it. It is like me, yet, it is not me. It is a bit unreal; you couldn't do very much with my shadow. Certainly without me it would be utterly useless. In fact, it wouldn't be what it was and it wouldn't be there. So that is a very good word and you may not know in the Greek language the word "true" and the word "real" are exactly the same word, so if you want to say something is real you say it is "true". If we wanted to say "God is for real" we would say, "God is true." If you think of that and then read John's Gospel again, "I am the truth" means "I am reality", "I am the true bread" means "I am the real bread". "In him all the promises are true" — they are real; "Yes and Amen".

So in fact what we are saying is that the Jewish religion is a bit unreal and we have got the real thing because we have got the true thing. It is this tabernacle that we are using, we are using the original. We could not worship if we were not using the real tabernacle, but we are using it in another place. Our High Priest is using the real tabernacle just as the High Priest of the Jews used theirs to relate them to God; ours is using the real one.

I want you therefore to realise that the tabernacle is not a thing of the past. I know the original Jewish model has long since faded, rotted, and gone back to the dust from which it was made but, having said that, the real tabernacle is still around, it is still being used — our High Priest is in the real one; he is in the holiest of holies now, and if he were not we could not worship God. So you are using the tabernacle. That is why we don't need a tabernacle-type building on earth; that is why we do not need a sanctuary here; that is why we do not need a holy place here. We have got a holy place, we only need a kind of convenient extension to the tabernacle for us to sit in. In fact, if somebody took away your church's building tomorrow and you had to meet in the open, you would still have all the building needed for true worship because you would still be using the true tabernacle.

Now I am emphasising this so that you get away from the idea that we have finished with all these things. We haven't— we are still using them but we are using the better ones. We are still using priesthood; we are still using a tabernacle, but we are using much better ones. They are not obsolete in that sense, but if you get the real thing you gladly throw away the copy. So that if I go away and take with me a photograph of my children then that is fine, it reminds me of them, but frankly when I come back home I can put it back in the drawer. I don't need it, I've got the real thing. Does that sort of give you the feel of the tabernacle? To summarise: there was a heavenly one and an earthly one and the heavenly one existed long before the earthly one; the heavenly one was the real one, and that is the real one that we are using now.

Consider the ground plan of that tabernacle for a moment. There was the big courtyard with the entrance. The big washing bowl, the altar where the main sacrifices were burned, with its four horns at the top, and then we come to an oblong building inside, divided into two. One beautifully embroidered curtain, and then the most richly embroidered curtain of all across the middle. You had a golden candlestick, a table of the showbread, and the altar of incense in the first room. Then right inside the second there was a chest with a lid on it, covered in gold. Inside were three things: two blocks of stone with the Ten Commandments engraved on them, which Moses brought from the mountain, Aaron's rod that budded, and a pot of manna to remind them how God gave them living bread. Then above: two angels. A chest, a bit like a linen chest covered with gold, a big slab on top which, covered with gold, was the mercy seat. Then you had two angels facing each other with wings—and all that in gold. One thing however that is striking is that in this first area, which was the holy place, where the priests could minister, there was a candlestick with candles on to light it, but there was neither window nor candle in the second — but if you had gone in it would have been too bright for you. Even though the whole of this box was covered with three layers of great sheets of different material, nevertheless this was the brightest part of the whole building because the glory of the Lord shone. So not only was there the gold itself, but the gold would reflect the glory, and if you went in it would be a dazzling display.

It is about this inner room that we are concerned because this dazzling glory, with the angels, is simply a copy. You see, in the real thing those angels are real, not carved. The whole thing is real and this is a copy, a magnificent copy. The women all brought their jewellery and rings, earrings to melt down for this gold. It must have been marvellous, but it is nothing compared with the real thing. Oh, one day you'll see the real thing with your eyes, and you will just be shattered at the beauty of it, and that is as it should be. So there are the earthly and the heavenly.

We are going to come back to the tabernacle later. We have been looking at the *premises*. Now we move on to the *promises*, because, way back, six hundred years before Jesus came, it was quite clear that the old covenant was a washout, it wasn't working, it was useless and ineffective.

Jeremiah himself foresaw that in fact even the covenant itself was a poor copy of the real one, would have to be replaced, and would become obsolete, antiquated, and left behind. So Jeremiah said there was a new covenant coming. Why didn't the older one work? There was nothing wrong with God's terms, there was nothing wrong with the conditions, nothing wrong with God's commandments, the laws. He said, "Here are the ten terms. Keep these ten words." This is the covenant not the contract. If it were a contract we might say to God, "Would six out of ten do? Maybe seven out of ten, I might manage that." But you see, it's not a contract. It's a covenant, Ten Commandments, you do the lot. Those are the terms. Those commandments are ideal for happy living. God didn't make commandments saying, "Thou shalt not," because he wanted to spoil our fun, but because he wanted us to live and know life. You break any of those, it is at your peril, and break one you have broken the lot. It is like a necklace of pearls: break one they scatter, and the seamless robe of righteousness just is torn up.

Nothing wrong with that covenant except that they just didn't keep the terms—they couldn't. They broke them, and the law had no real provision for deliberate breaking of commandments. It had provision for sins of ignorance, but it had no provision for a man who had deliberately, consciously, wilfully broken those commandments. That was one of the problems, and it was a very real problem. So it didn't work and Jeremiah promised a new one.

The terms of the new covenant are marvellous; the terms are fourfold. First, that it would be a covenant with the Law written inside people and not outside them. As long as they are carved on tablets of stone they are outside you and that is the problem—if they could only be written inside you. A simple illustration I have used before comes back to my mind. A mother said, "My teenage boy, I have tried for ten years to get him to brush his hair, put on a clean shirt and polish his shoes, and I just can't do it. Now suddenly, within three weeks he's brushing his hair, putting on a clean shirt every day, and polishing his shoes." Now, what has happened to that boy? Something has been written on his heart and she found out who the girl was pretty soon. Now you see, instead of writing up on his wall to stick in his bedroom, "Thou shalt put a clean shirt on every morning," it is now written on his heart and he wants a clean shirt every morning. Do you see the difference? Now that is the first term of the new covenant.

The commandments are still going to be written, make no mistake about it. Whoever tries to say that Christianity has less strict standards than Judaism is not reading the New Testament. Jesus said something pretty strong about those who relaxed a single commandment. No — Christians, if anything, have a stricter standard to live by because Jesus said that the commandments apply to your inside life not just the outside. This is the new covenant — the first thing, "I will write them into their hearts."

The second thing is that there will be a relationship with God. If you try to keep the commandments without the relationship that is a real problem. What writes the law on your heart is the fact that you are in a relationship of love with someone. "They will all know me...." A personal experience of God, not a distant experience where a priest goes somewhere on your behalf and tells you what he has seen and what he has experienced, but *I* can have a experience of God. Now I will know him personally so it is not only inward, it is experiential too.

Thirdly, it will give me a personal knowledge of God—I will know him and I won't need to be taught. It is great when you move from a secondhand knowledge of God to a firsthand knowledge of him. The new covenant is not just about sending hymns and prayers up to God, but about *knowing* him.

The fourth part of this new covenant is that it will deal with the root problem of guilt, for which the old law made no real provision. It will deal with the person who has broken every commandment, and broken them terribly. It will deal with that by the simple expedient of including forgiveness in the terms. The new covenant is based upon forgiveness — not only forgiving but forgetting, because if you haven't forgotten a thing, you haven't forgiven it. The problem is that we human beings find it very difficult to forgive someone else because we can't forget. But the marvellous thing is that God has total control over his own memory. To me the greatest shock will be when one gets to heaven and says, "Lord, looking back now I'm so sorry about that," and he will say, "About what?"

"But Lord, don't you remember that?"

"No, I don't remember that."

"Well I do."

"There is no need for you to because I have forgotten it. Your sins I will remember no more."

What a covenant! When we come to the communion table we come to remember the blood of the covenant shed for you and for many, for the remission of sins. It is still all part of the same religious system — covenant, sacrifice, blood, atonement, it is all there, and yet how much better not to have to do all those things that the Jews had to do because we have got the real thing. So the old covenant is obsolete.

We have looked at Christ being the minister of a better covenant, now we look at him as being not just the minister who serves but the Mediator who goes in between— Mediator of a blood covenant. This word "blood" is vital; it occurs eleven times in this next section. I don't know if you like blood, or if you are one of those who faint at the sight of blood—if you do you would never have stood at the worship of the Jews. The wine used at communion is deliberately put there as the colour of blood to make you look on it and think of blood because we are going to see now that *the fundamental principle is that but for blood you could not have your guilt removed, you could not be forgiven*.

Let us look again at the premises in heaven. Remember that the Jews had a visible sanctuary, a visible tabernacle, a visible building. Some people say, "Well, wasn't that a help to them?" Yes, it was. It was a kind of living visual aid. "Well, wouldn't it be a help to us?" No, it wouldn't, because the tragedy is that if you have this kind of visual aid, if you have a sanctuary type of building, then your attention is more and more on earth, and you come to depend on an earthly building instead of by faith depending on the heavenly. That is why I believe churches should not look like sanctuaries; they should be tidy, they should be compatible with wholesomeness, they should be nicely designed, but they should not attempt to be a sanctuary. Otherwise, if you are not careful, you will get the feeling as you might when you go into any cathedral, that God is up at one end. Have you had that feeling? But we have boldness — to come boldly to the throne of grace. We want to get as near as possible because we don't look at any earthly sanctuary; we are looking at the invisible premises. It is by faith that you can see them. Can you just look at them now? — If you like, close your eyes. Look, and see that heavenly tabernacle. Can you see your High Priest right in the brightest part of it? Jesus Christ is right there, so we have something much better.

In the visible tabernacle you saw that colour red everywhere. You saw it sprinkled, you would see it all over the mercy seat and you see it running down. Get that colour fixed in your mind — it is all the way through. Why? Because it is a *bloody* business getting through to God. I am putting it as strongly as that so you won't forget. The reason is very simple: because sin is the most expensive thing in the world. You cannot pay for it with money; you can only pay for it with life given in death. It costs someone's blood every time you sin. The tragedy is that unless you allow Jesus Christ to pay, you will pay for it with your own blood. You will have to — the bill comes in and the bill is death.

The cheap view of forgiveness is that all that is needed is a pat on the head, and saying, "Boys will be boys; Ah, forget it." That is not forgiveness because there isn't any blood in it. Even with the old way, the high priest had to take blood for his own sins and for other people's; he went in to take blood all the way. He did not dare to go anywhere near God unless there was blood in front of God. That's right, and if you don't understand why it is necessary, then you don't understand God's holiness yet. You don't understand how pure he is if you don't realise what sin costs in terms of the bill that needs to be paid. All the money in the world could not afford one sin that you have committed—not one. It costs more than that.

So in the old, visible tabernacle the high priest came in with a bowl of blood and would sprinkle people and things all the way in—sprinkle himself for he had to, he needed it as much as they did. Because he needed it, he had to keep well away from God most of the time. Remember that only he got into there, and only once a year. Even then the blood only cleansed them ceremonially, it didn't deal with their conscience, which is why they were back the next day to offer something else.

It is a fact that if all you have got is religion, your conscience never gets clear so you keep coming back with a bit more religion. You may go through all the motions, you may worship to the best of your sincerity, and you go home with a guilty conscience and it has not been cleansed and that is the real problem. I may be outwardly, ceremonially clean, but it hasn't dealt with my guilt problem that I can't live with this memory. There is only one thing that will deal with that and it is not the blood of bulls and goats, it is the blood of our Lord Jesus Christ, because it is the only blood of a sacrifice that was voluntary, rational and obedient, and not just the blood of an innocent animal.

You see the difference between men and animals can be said to be precisely this: man has a conscience. How, therefore, can the blood of an animal who has never had a conscience atone for a man with a guilty conscience? This was the actual hard fact that the Old Testament saints, however saintly, kept coming back with — more sacrifices because they just couldn't get things off their conscience — and then came Jesus. He entered into those premises in heaven, having offered his blood on earth. You know the remarkable thing is, as the letter to the Hebrews says here: if Jesus were on earth now he would not be eligible to be a priest. Do you realise that? He could not be your priest because he is not eligible, he is not of the tribe of Levi, he is of the tribe of Judah. Thank God he is in heaven; he became my High Priest when he went back there and became eligible on a totally different ground.

Now the letter to the Hebrews does not say that he has taken the blood into heaven. He left his blood on earth; he has not taken that in. He has taken in pierced hands, pierced feet, and a gashed side, and he shows those to the Father. The blood has been shed, sacrifice has been made; it is never repeated, it is not going on at the moment, it is finished. That is why, unlike the priests, when he went in he sat down. As much as to say, "I've finished the work and I'm sitting down at the end of the day." So he went in not to stand and offer repeated sacrifices, he went in to sit.

This is, therefore, in a sense, a living sacrifice. Notice

the contrast, "more perfect, not made with hands, once for all" — as against once a year. What a lovely contrast in those phrases, "His own blood", not the blood of bulls and goats, "eternal redemption", therefore never to be repeated. Therefore, it is a very practical thing, and the practical result is: cleansing from dead works and turning to the living God. No other sacrifice in the world can achieve that practical result of getting a man away from dead works and to the living God. None of the Old Testament sacrifices ever did it.

Now go right back to that word "covenant" at the beginning. If you have made your will, you'll notice that the word "covenant" is sometimes used in the will.

Looking at my own Will, I thought: as a bit of paper it is absolutely useless and valueless until one thing happens —when I die. Then suddenly the covenant that I have set my name to becomes effective. However wonderful it may be, until that moment occurs, whatever expectations others may have, nothing happens until my heart stops beating. In that moment, that piece of paper becomes all-important.

The covenant which God said he would make through Jeremiah — 600 years before Christ — took effect the day Jesus said, "It is finished" —and as soon as he breathed his last. The Will came into operation; the provisions happened and, ever since, those who have been to the cross have found that the covenant is an actual fact of experience; that my sins can be forgiven and forgotten; that I can know God personally; that I can have his Law written on my heart. Not outside or up on my wall, but in my heart which is where it is far more important. That is where you need the Word of God written.

A testament (and that is another word for covenant—it is the same word) is of no effect until blood has been shed. Therefore, by inference, the new covenant based on forgiveness means simply this: there cannot ever be forgiveness without shedding of blood. That is the most serious thought, and the reason why we take communion regularly is simply lest we forget the cost of forgiveness, lest we, with our easy "forgive and forget" attitude to ourselves and to other people, should forget what it cost Christ to forgive us.

> He died that we might be forgiven,
> he died to make us good,
> that we might go at last to heaven,
> Saved by his precious blood.

Or as Isaac Watts put it,

> Not all the blood of beasts
> On Jewish altars slain,
> Could give the guilty conscience peace,
> Or wash away the stain.

> But Christ the Heavenly Lamb,
> Takes all our sins away;
> A sacrifice of nobler name,
> And richer blood than they.

So we turn from the shadows to the substance, from the unreal to the real, from the copies to the true, from the earthly to the heavenly, from the present evil age to the age to come, which has already dawned in our hearts by faith. The point of all that we are saying is this: we have such a High Priest, his majesty in heaven, on the throne of God, who serves there in the real tabernacle.

7

BETTER SANCTUARY
Read 9:23 – 10:39

A. HIS SINGLE SACRIFICE (9:23–10:18)
1. Appearance – timeliness (9:23–28)
2. Obedience – willingness (10:1–10)
3. Eminence – forgiveness (10:11–18)
B. OUR SURE SANCTUARY (10:19–39)
1. Confidence – togetherness (19–25)
2. Perseverance – wilfulness (26–31)
3. Endurance – faithfulness ((32–39)

We have seen that we have better premises and better promises than the Jews ever had. Indeed this word "better" is the key word of the letter to the Hebrews. There is something more we are going to develop now in more detail. Our religion is better because ours is a heavenly religion; the Jewish religion was an earthly one. They had to make do with copies of the real thing. It is very important that we should get right the true relationship between the Old Testament and the New Testament. It is all part of the Bible and Christians read both, but how to relate them is a very delicate judgment.

On the one hand, there are those who take the Old Testament at its face value, and assume that its provisions must be observed by Christians, and we find Christians pleading for Sabbath observance, which is a real contradiction in terms. On the other hand, we get those who just simply dismiss the Old Testament as out of date, and say, "Well, my

Christianity is based on the New Testament." Both of those two positions are over-simplified. God wants us to have his whole Word but to relate the two testaments rightly.

There is a little doggerel line: "The old is in the new revealed; the new is in the old concealed." This points out the very important principle that the Old Testament has not been just dismissed; it has not been abolished in one tiny detail, not one jot or one tittle of the Mosaic Law has been abolished. But, on the other hand, we don't observe the Mosaic Law because its principles are now applied in a far better way. It has not been abolished; it has been fulfilled. Christ has shed his blood once and for all and cleansed not only earth but even heaven itself with his blood.

One day in the prayer time before a service, when our elders were praying, one of them prayed that Christ would sprinkle blood on every part of the service. We believe that he has done so and that we go through a blood-sprinkled act of worship. There is blood on the songs we sing; there is blood on the prayers we pray; there is blood on the sermon. All the way through, there is blood. If there wasn't, we could not get anywhere near God. It is the only cleansing agent that we know of that is able to get rid of stains in the heart. Water certainly won't.

This was the message of the tabernacle, "Don't come near me," said God, "unless you bring blood, unless you bring evidence of a life that's been taken, an innocent life; don't come near me because I could not accept you until that's happened." So all the way in from the gate to the most holy place, blood all the way. You see, we haven't finished with this, we have just transformed it. It has not been abolished but fulfilled, and it is by the blood of Jesus and that is why we sing about it.

The reason we modern people have an aversion to blood is that we think physical hygiene is more important than spiritual, and we are so wrong. Jesus was once criticised for not washing his hands before a meal and he said, "Look, the important thing is the dirt in your heart at this meal table and what comes out of your mouth this meal time, not what goes in.

We get so worried about physical hygiene that if we started sprinkling blood about the church building you would feel it was making it dirty. But, in fact, in God's sight, you could be making it clean—what a big difference between God's outlook and ours. So blood is there in the Old and the New Testament. "Washed in the blood of the Lamb" would be a phrase that a Jew could understand, probably even better than a Christian, because all the tradition of the shadows, the visual aids, the lessons in bricks, stones, wood and linen, were there in his history.

I have divided this passage into two halves: something about Christ and then something about us. The first half is a study of principle, the second a study of practice; the first half a study of belief, the second a study of behaviour. So often the New Testament is like this — it lifts you up in principle and belief and then it brings you down to earth with a bump and says, "Now practise it in your behaviour." The balance is beautiful because what you believe affects your behaviour. If you believed it was going to rain this morning, you would have taken an umbrella or worn a raincoat!

So let's look first at belief and if it sounds a little theoretical you just wait until we get to the practical and see what implications it has. *His single sacrifice* is the principle we are going to look at and *our sure sanctuary* is the practice of that principle.

His sacrifice. I don't know if you realise that heaven got dirty with sin. We tend to think it is all on earth and that this planet is the only place where there is sin, and any Sunday newspaper will tell you all about it. But this is not the only place where there is sin, and we need to realise that heaven got polluted as well as planet earth, and that there is moral pollution in God's own presence in heaven.

The proof of it is that as soon as you get through to heaven, as soon as you get into contact, you will find evil. As soon as you are in the heavenly places in Christ Jesus you will find that you are wrestling not against flesh and blood on earth, but against principalities, powers, spiritual hosts of wickedness. Where? In the heavenly places—things went wrong up there as well as down here and the blood of Jesus had to cleanse the whole universe. Not just little earth, but he had to cleanse the heavenlies as well as the earthly, and this is what he has done. When Christ's blood was shed and the blood and water flowed from his side, not only was earth getting cleaned up, but heaven was too.

The emphasis when we read the passage at the end of chapter nine is the contrast between all the sacrifices they put on that altar and the one single sacrifice that Jesus put on the altar. They had to keep on doing it. They knew in their hearts that it was not working. If you keep going back to the chemist for the same bottle of medicine, if you keep going back to the doctor with the same complaint, you are admitting openly that you are not cured and that you are no better.

They came day after day, year after year, month after month, to put a sacrifice on that altar, and once a year the High Priest, as he was allowed to do, went into that inner room, with blood—not his own because his own was tainted, but the blood of a pure animal. If he kept going in year after year after year, didn't that underline that it wasn't working? There is a remarkable phrase in the book of Numbers where it says that the sacrifices of those days were a remembrance of sin. In other words, every time they offered it, it reminded them that they still had sin. Holy Communion could not be more different from those sacrifices because Holy

Communion is not a reminder of your sin but a reminder of your salvation. You see the difference? We repeat it not because we feel that sin has not been dealt with, but we just want to praise and thank God that it *has* been dealt with. It becomes a thank you service. The Greek for "thank you" is *eucharisto* and we call it a Eucharist because it is saying thank you not for a reminder of sin but for a reminder of our salvation. So we don't call Holy Communion a sacrifice, it is so different. Jesus did it once and it was finished. Among his last words were, "It is finished." No High Priest who offered other sacrifices ever made such a statement.

Therefore, while the High Priest used to go on standing, Jesus sat down. Go out for an evening meal and if you see certain people sitting at the table and certain people standing around, you can assume that certain people have finished their work and certain people haven't. The people sitting at the table are finished for the day; the people standing around them have not. They are going on serving. This very standing and sitting posture underlines the same thing — that Jesus when he had hung on a cross sat down later — finished; no more sacrifices.

There are three *appearances* of Christ mentioned. First: his present appearance before the Father. He doesn't keep coming and going to God. He appeared before the Father once to pray for us. That is where he is now. He has appeared before the Father where he holds up the nailprints — hands never to be pierced again. Second: his appearance when he appeared on earth. Why did he appear on earth? So that he might be killed for us and shed his blood. Third: the appearance of Jesus at the end of the world when he will come for a totally different purpose.

These are the three appearances and each of them is a one-off appearance. None is repeated because the purposes are different and therefore the appearances are different.

It is appointed to man to die once and then you will see your neighbour again once more. It is a sobering thought that you will see everybody you knew once more — and they will appear a second time but for a very different purpose. They appeared on earth to do God's will, and they will appear a second time to be accounted for, as to whether they did it. So everybody who has appeared once on earth will appear once more for judgment.

Christ, having appeared once on earth to do God's will, will appear once more not to be judged as he was on his first visit, but to judge. On that day Pontius Pilate will see him again but the roles will be reversed. Annas and Caiaphas will see him again but the roles will be reversed. Herod will see him again, the roles reversed.

So Jesus Christ only came to earth once to sacrifice for sins and he will come once again for judgment. In between he has appeared in heaven. Once for all — whereas if you had been at the tabernacle, you would have seen the priest — he kept going in, coming out; appearing, disappearing. It just went on and on and was getting nowhere.

The second theme mentioned in this first half of the passage is Jesus' obedience. The whole business of sacrifice was only a pale copy and the reason is very simple. In the Old Testament (have you ever read it with this in mind?) there is a tension between: does God want sacrifices and blood, or does he want obedience? The tension grows as you go through the Old Testament. You get, for example, that statement in Samuel, "To obey is better than sacrifice." Oh, does that mean that obedience can be a substitute for sacrifice? You find it in Isaiah, the same note sounded. You find it in Hosea, in Amos, in Micah 6:6, all through the Prophets, this tension. What does God want? In Psalm 51 it is there. David cries out in confession and says, "I know you don't want offering and sacrifices, burnt offerings and the blood of bulls and goats.... I know you want the sacrifice of a broken and a contrite heart."

Which does God want? Does he want sacrifices or obedience? The tension is there and scholars have argued about it. Some say, "Well, sacrifice at first, and then obedience replaced it." Some say, "No." The big debate goes on. There is a very simple answer to it. The tension in the Old Testament is there because God wanted both, and he could never get them in the Old Testament. He could never get a sacrifice of blood that represented an obedient life. If you had seen those poor little lambs being dragged to that altar, you would not have seen any obedience there. God was waiting for blood of an obedient life. The High Priest wasn't obedient enough to offer his own blood. Nobody was.

There is this tension until you get to the New Testament. At the end of Psalm 51, David realises that once God has a broken and a contrite heart, and an obedient heart — *then* I will offer to you the sacrifice. He realised that God wants *both*. When Jesus came, he said, "Lord, I've come to do your will" and he fulfilled the scripture: you have given me a body so that I can provide my own sacrifice of an obedient, rational offering. For the first time blood was shed not only of someone who volunteered to shed it, but who lived a perfectly obedient life before he offered it. Therefore, for the first time, sacrifice and obedience blended. A man prayed with drops of blood on his brow, "Not my will but thine be done." Oh, we have a better sacrifice. Not an unwilling animal dragged as if to an abattoir, but a Son who set his face to go to Jerusalem and who refused to let his servants even wield a sword for him, and who went to die.

The third thing is the *eminence* that Jesus has. We have already mentioned this manner of standing and sitting down. The priest was doing it daily; the Lord did it once and for all, but the emphasis here is that he can sit down because he achieved at last what sacrifice was meant to do. What sacrifice was meant to do was take away sin, not just to get it overlooked. Throughout the Old Testament, it says that God covered sin over; their sins were covered by the blood of the sacrifices. But do you know what Jesus does? He doesn't just cover it; he removes it. "Blessed is the Lamb of God who *takes away*...." He doesn't paper it over. You can cover a thing up or you can remove it. Which is best? The sacrifices of the Old Testament only covered things over for the time being, never rooted them out.

It is like digging weeds into your garden. You try digging them in and covering it over with nice clean soil. You see if that deals with the problem. In fact, it multiplies it. You need to take them away, and get rid of them, remove the stuff, and then your soil is clean. The *eminence* of Jesus Christ is that he didn't come to cover it up. God had been covering things up for a long time. In fact, in one text in the New Testament it says of the Jews that God had winked at their sins. He had overlooked them, but that's not enough. I need a sacrifice that will take them away.

Once I get a sacrifice that can take them away, I am finished with sacrifice. Do you see? There is no more offering for sin; there is nothing more to be done because the root has been taken away. The thing has been dealt with. There is no need to keep covering it over any more. It has gone and that is the eminence of our Lord's sacrifice. It has achieved a forgiveness that all the other sacrifices did not achieve. They covered things over from God's sight; Jesus' sacrifice removed, took away, put away. These are the phrases used here—very strong language.

Let us come to the second half: a surer sanctuary. v. 19. "Therefore brothers..." and everything now is addressed to Christians. If you are not a Christian, I haven't any word for you now. All the rest of chapter ten is to Christian brothers.

There is an exhortation, a severe warning, and a practical appeal. This pattern of exhortation—warning—appeal has already occurred, in Hebrews 6. It is a favourite pattern that is good preaching, balanced Word of God. To exhort people to do something, give them a severe warning of what happens if they don't do it, and appeal to them strongly because of the reward which comes if they do do it. So those are the three points I want to deal with now.

What we are saying is this: there is a human side to all this, as well as the divine. Christ has done, once for all, all that needs to be done. But if we are going to enjoy the results of it there is a continual thing that we need to do. Now how often we get it the other way round. How often we say, "Jesus should do something continually for me because I once for all trusted him." Jesus has done everything once for all; it is we who must have the continuous attitude to him. So we have this exhortation: "Let us...." The exhortation is in the continuous present tense, which means, "Let us go on doing something." He has once for all done everything that is needed, so let us continually do something.

What must we do? Faith, hope and love. This is our side: Let us draw near with full assurance of faith; let's hold fast to our hope, and let's provoke one another to love.

He has once for all taken away sin. That does not mean that we are in practice sinless yet. The Bible is honest, it says, listen to this, "By his one sacrifice he has made perfect forever those who are being made holy." Now isn't that honest? Do you get the double aspect? He has made perfect forever those who are being made holy. In other words, God already sees the finished product when he looks at your life. He has made you perfect forever, so he is making you holy now.

Isn't that lovely? The word "perfect" here means "complete, whole," and that is what "holy" means. He has made you complete in Christ. It is all there, once and for all. You have all you need in Christ. Nothing needs to be added to his work; it is all there so he is making you whole because he has already made you complete — and that is the tension of the Christian life. We know we have everything in Christ but we are still trying to appropriate it. So let us come with faith.

A person can come with boldness, without fear. He can come in full assurance — there should be no room for doubt. I would be worried if my children doubted whether I loved them. Your Heavenly Father is far more worried if you doubt whether he loves you, "Oh you of little faith" is how Jesus talked. How much more will he love you? Care for you? Give you? So we are to come with full assurance of faith, having our conscience clean — that is vital — having had our bodies washed in pure water. If you have not been baptised you will be lacking in full assurance because baptism is part of giving you the full assurance. So we approach with our bodies washed in pure water, our conscience free, and Peter in his letter links the two when he speaks of baptism as not being a washing of dirt from the body but an appeal to God for a clean conscience. So the washing of the body in clean water brings about the clean conscience, which brings full assurance of faith to draw near. That is the first thing to do — get as near to God as you can. Everything has been done by Christ, so get as near to God as you can.

You can get very near because the way is wide open. Again remember how in the past nobody could get near God, he lived in an inside room and only the High Priest could go in there once a year. This seemed to say more clearly than anything else that God is so near and yet so far. He was right there in the middle of the camp, in his own tent, but you can't go in and meet him. But now, let us with full assurance of faith go right into the holy place, right in to the Holy of

Holies and talk to our Father—the privilege of access.

Second, let us hold fast our hope. This is part of it too. Our confidence must have an anchor, out of sight. The chain may be visible but the anchor is out of sight. Unlike most anchors on earth, this one is above, not below. An anchor within the true veil, covering the real Holy of holies.

Third, let us stir each other up. Literally, let's irritate each other to love. Now, I find this a little difficult to expound. We are good at provoking one another to hatred, not so good at *irritating* each other to love. The word means to prick each other to love, to goad each other, to nag each other to love. Notice a most important thing here. Away with the individualism of *my personal search* for holiness — the Bible says: "Stir one another up to love." You see, if you try to make love a private quest of your own, it will defeat its own object because love cannot be developed that way. Your personal concern should not so much be with your loving but stirring others up to love, and they will stir you up. In other words, your concern should be the holiness of the fellowship. Immediately there is put in a very healthy emphasis: Therefore, don't neglect meetings at church. Don't forsake the assembling together. If you are going to help others to be holy you have got to be there.

Jesus has done everything he needs to do. Let us draw near with faith, let us hold fast our hope, and let us irritate one another to love. Mind you, we need to qualify that, don't we? You can so irritate people that you think you are giving them the most marvellous opportunity to be patient, loving, and kind, but that is not what is meant here.

So, in this second half: first, *confidence*. The veil has been ripped. It was a gorgeously embroidered curtain, but it was ripped from the top to the bottom which means God's hands ripped it. If I can put it this way: when Jesus died, God was uncovered. God was exposed when Jesus died. The veil was ripped, and it was ripped at the very moment that his body was ripped. That veil was in a sense a symbol of his flesh because God was in Christ, but the veil was there and people could look at him and say, "Is not this the carpenter's son?" They didn't see, but when he died the veil was ripped and people saw God. If you want to know what God is like, look at Jesus on the cross. You can see now what God is like, and he is holiness and love. The veil is gone, rendering obsolete the temple and the tabernacle, but exposing God and saying come right in. Let us draw near.

The second note in our sure sanctuary is *perseverance*. There is something serious in 10:26–31. It is all of a piece with Hebrews 6, and it is addressed to Christians. If you have come to knowledge of a single sacrifice to take away sin, but you go on in a state of mind that simply wants it covered up but not taken away, then frankly you put yourself in a very dangerous position. If you treat the sacrifice of Christ in the same way as if it were the same as the sacrifice in the tabernacle, then you are in frightful and fearful danger. If you just want things covered up but not removed, what are you doing? There are three strong words listed here. You are *spurning* the Son of God, you are *profaning* the Heavenly Father, and you are *outraging* the Spirit of grace. Those are very strong verbs, expressing horror. The Lord knows, if people insult us as much as they can, they still don't know the worst about us. But when you do it to the Son of God, when you outrage the Spirit of grace, which you do if you don't want sins taken away — in other words, as the writer says, "If you go on wilfully sinning after you found out about this one sacrifice..." what are you doing? You are putting yourself beyond reach because this one sacrifice is the only one there is. It is once for all and there is nothing else. Therefore, if you don't let this one work in your life there is nothing else that will work, and there is nothing for you to look forward to but a fearful judgment and a raging fire. Then comes this severe word, which is in the New Testament not the Old, and which is written for believers not unbelievers: "It is a fearful thing to fall into the hands of the living God." How do you fall into them? Very simply, those fall into the hands of the living God who haven't come into them. You either come into them with full assurance of faith and say, "Thou blessed rock of ages, I'm hiding in thee," or else you are hiding from him and from others in which case, there will one day be nowhere to hide—that is the severe warning given here. There is the need for perseverance, the need for letting the sacrifice that Christ made once for all really work and do its job. He sat down in heaven expecting the sacrifice to work, just waiting until all his enemies are under his feet. He knows it has got to work; he knows it is going to work, and it will. One day, every enemy of Christ will be under his feet—his footstool. But whether an individual lets it work fully or not is a different question. The writer here warns us that if we have got a better sacrifice then it must do a better job with us than the old ones did with the Jews.

Finally, there is a plea for *endurance*. They have been having a tough time already and the words hint of the Roman arena, I think. "You have suffered affliction" or literally, "You have had to fight." Believers had been imprisoned, and if they didn't go to prison themselves at least they went to visit Christians who were in prison, identifying with them. Does that challenge us to identify a little more with our brethren who are in prison? They lost their possessions. Should we be willing to identify more with them?

One church of which I was pastor, in their church records I found out that there were days when the Baptists in that village had their property confiscated by the public authorities, their furniture, their goods and chattels, and they had to watch all their private possessions being sold on the village green in Chalfont St. Peter. The proceeds were not given back to them and then they were hauled off to Aylesbury Jail, but they went singing hymns. Why? Because they had far better possessions. Someone in my congregation was burgled and I will never forget their first remark: "The thieves couldn't touch our most treasured possessions." You can stand the loss of everything if you have something better that can't be touched, "...where moth and rust do not consume, and thieves do not break through and steal." So there are these words: You have already known persecution. You lost your property gladly. Don't give up now please.

This is the appeal he makes: "There's a reward waiting for you and it's only a little while longer. Fancy just not enduring, and losing the reward at this late stage." Now the writer of this letter clearly knew a lot about sailing. In nautical terms: you have been through the worst of the storm, don't reef your sails now when the voyage is nearly over. It is a tremendous appeal and he uses the Greek term for reefing your sails, bringing them down a bit, "shrinking back" it is usually translated here – a naval term for lowering sail.

He says: I beg you, the voyage is nearly over, just a little while more ... the just shall live by faith. The rescuer is on his way. He will come and he won't be late. The date is already fixed and the time is known to God when Jesus is coming back to complete it all. Hang on until the end of the voyage. Hold to the anchor. Don't drift. Complete the voyage, don't shrink back; don't lower your sails; don't lose heart, but endure ... right on to the end. We are not of those who shrink back and are destroyed, who lower their sails and stop sailing, but of those who go on believing and are saved.

8

WHAT FAITH IS AND DOES
Read 11:1 – 12:2

A. FAITH EXPLAINED (11:1–3)
1. Assurance of the future (1)
2. Approval of the present (2)
3. Appearance of the past (8)
B. FAITH EXEMPLIFIED (11:4–40)
1. Pioneers and pilgrims (4–12)
    a. Abel (4)
    b. Enoch (5–6)
    c. Noah (7)
    d. Abraham/Sarah (8–12)
2. A better country (13–16)
3. Patriarchs and prophets ((17–38)
    a. Abraham (17–19) b. Isaac (20)
    c. Jacob (21) d. Joseph (22)
    e. Moses (23–29) f. Joshua/Rahab (30–31)
    g. Gideon, Samson, Barak, Jephthah, David,
       Samuel, prophets, etc. (32)
        i. Conquests of faith (33–34)
        ii. Costs of faith (35–37)
4. A better community (39–40)
C. FAITH EXERCISED (12:1–2)
1. Witnesses from the past (1a)
2. Weights in the present (1b)
3. Winners of the future (2)

Chapter 11 is the best-known chapter of the whole letter to the Hebrews. But it is often read in isolation, separated from all that has gone before and all that comes after it. Thereby it loses a great deal of its meaning. Now we can put it back into context because we have been studying this letter chapter by chapter.

We come now to something else Christianity has that is better than they had in the Old Testament. We not only have a better leader, a better sanctuary, a better High Priest, a better sacrifice, we also have a better *country*. It is that better country, which we believe in and to which we are travelling in faith. But you know it comes as a shock to realise that believers in the Old Testament days were not content with the land of Canaan. They too looked beyond it for a better country. They too believed in a New Jerusalem, not just the old one. They too shared the faith which we have in Christ.

There is a connection therefore between all that has gone before and this chapter. The better things of which we have spoken are all invisible. Most of our knowledge comes to us through our five senses—sight, hearing, touch, taste, smell. But none of these better things is available to any of the five senses. Therein is our problem. That is why people want priests on earth and that is why they want a sanctuary on earth. They want something down here so that they can see and feel and handle. But the people whom God commends are those who see the invisible, those who are as certain of the things they cannot see and touch as of those things that are tangible. Those who walk by faith are those who are absolutely certain of things that nobody else can see. Faith is the very substance of those things. Faith is the tangible thing to us. I can feel my faith, I know that there is faith right here, and that is the tangible evidence of things that I cannot see.

Do you realise that we are in the same position as Abraham, in a sense, towards the resurrection? He didn't see it; we didn't see it. He believed that God could raise the dead and would; we believe that God could raise the dead and did. But we have to have the same faith. So those before and after the events of the death and resurrection of Jesus have to share the same faith because neither can see these things. Thomas spoke for many people when he said, "Until I can push my finger through the hole in his hands and thrust my hand into his side, I won't believe". That is the scientific approach *par excellence*—modern scepticism summed up two thousand years ago. Jesus very graciously, because he needed that man Thomas to start his church, said: Alright then, you can handle and see. But blessed are those who have not seen but have believed... Abraham rejoiced to see my day and was glad. Abraham saw his day? How long before? Nearly two thousand years before, and Abraham saw it. So we are going to look at this matter of faith. First of all, we explain faith, then faith is given to us in examples, then we are told how to exercise it.

We have first of all the *explanation* of faith—what it is. It is faith that has given us our passport to another country, given us our rights of citizenship, given us authority to look up and say to God, "Abba, Dad!" There have been many explanations or definitions of faith. One of the worst was from a schoolboy who was asked by his RE teacher, "What is faith?" He said, "It's believing what you know isn't true." The world thinks that is what we are doing as Christians — that we are crazy, that we are trying to kid ourselves, that we have brainwashed ourselves into believing something that isn't true.

Here is the biblical definition, "Now faith is being sure of what we hoped for...." The word "hope" in the English vocabulary is a very uncertain word, full of speculation and doubt. Is it going to snow tomorrow? My children say, "I hope so," but they are not sure; I say, "I hope not," but I'm

143

not sure either. When we say, "I hope" — "I hope I live to a good old age; I hope I'll have health and strength; I hope I'll never be left lonely; I hope I won't suffer from this disease," I hope, I hope, I hope — it is all so uncertain and shaky. It is really "I wish", but the word "hope" in the Bible is a strong word, so strong that it is said to be an anchor within the veil, and anchors are not built weak. They are built strong, rigid and robust. Faith is being sure of what you hoped for.

If somebody says, "Are you going to heaven?" don't say, "I hope so," because that's using the word in an English sense. Say, "I'm absolutely certain of it."

"Oh, does that mean you're better than I am?"

"No, it doesn't mean anything of the kind. It just means that God is a good deal better than you think."

What else is faith? It is the certainty of what we do not see. To be as certain of what you cannot see as of what you can is faith and it is a gift of God. You can't work it up. You can't brainwash yourself into believing, you just can't do it. If you do, it is shaky, and at the first big test it will collapse. When God has given you the genuine article, that faith is certain of things not seen.

You see, therefore, that faith has a relationship to the future. It also has some bearing on the present. Faith is what God commends people for. If you want to know who God accepts, who is in God's good books—that's a good, simple paraphrase of the word "justified" in scripture—who is in God's good books? Who does God commend? Who does God think highly of? — I tell you, it is those who believe now; those who are not going to say, "I'll wait and see how it turns out," but who say, "I'm going to believe now. I have faith now." These are the people God commends.

But faith also can go back into the past and can go further back than science can. In a sense, faith goes further forward than human thinking can take us, further up than human thinking can take us, and further back than human thinking can take us. It goes further forward because it is sure of things not yet seen and still future. It goes further up because it is sure that God commends those who believe. It goes further back, too — whereas science is utterly dependent on observation and of making evidence available to the senses in some way — whether it be microscope, radio telescope, or whatever. No-one can tell us the truth or the untruth of the first ten words of the Bible. They are a statement that go further into the past than science can take us. "In the beginning God created the heavens and the earth...." It is by faith that we believe that something was made out of nothing. It is by faith that we believe God simply had to speak and matter and energy began to be. It is only by faith you can believe that. Faith is not contrary to true reason or reason based on truth, but it goes so much further. That is why reason alone can never believe. That is why you can never argue anyone into faith. You may remove some of the intellectual barriers they have, and that needs to be done with some. That is why people who have a strong faith appear to the world as dogmatic, because they are so sure. It is not that they are sure of themselves. I am afraid we sometimes give that impression. People have sometimes said to me, "You seem so sure of yourself when you speak." I'm not sure of myself, if you only knew. But I am sure of God, and I am sure of heaven, and I am sure of creation. I am absolutely certain of these things, so I am prepared to preach them dogmatically, not just engage in discussion, but state what I am sure of. Now that is faith.

So let us now turn from the *explanation* of faith to see some *examples*. You can always understand it better if you look at specific examples. Truth in the Bible is personal. It does not come to us as a book of philosophy or science. It is not a systematic book of theology. Thank God it isn't. It comes to us in life. It comes to us in people. It comes to us in real situations, flesh and blood, people such as we are and that is the glory of the Bible. You are not asked to believe an encyclopedia, you are asked to look at people. Supremely, as we shall see, you are asked to take your mind off even the people we are going to look at, and look to Jesus. One person —if you look to him that is enough to have faith.

Now there is nothing at all new about faith, it is an old record. Maybe this is why the modern world finds it difficult to listen to these accounts, but it is as old as the first family. If Adam was the first man who lost his faith, then his son was the first man who found it. We start therefore the story of faith with Abel. It has been said that if we will not learn from history then we are condemned to relive it. If we are not prepared to look back over the past and learn from those who have walked with God through the centuries then, alas, we shall have to learn their lessons all over again.

What a joy it is when the Lord deals with your pride in such a way, especially when you are young, when you think you know better than everybody else, and your parents are so old-fashioned it is unbelievable. Isn't it wonderful when the Lord humbles you and says, "Look at the past. Look at the great heroes of the faith." I was deeply moved when a young man came to me and asked if he could borrow to read some books about lives some of the saints of old. I think I gave him about half a dozen books of different saints, men who have long since died. No wonder the Lord has called him into his service. He was looking back over the cloud of witnesses and learning from them. Let us do the same.

God's honours list is far more important than any national honours list. God's list is the one you want to get your name on. These are the ones God commends. First of all, we look at some of the pioneers and pilgrims of the earliest days. Notice that they are all treated as real individuals — and then there are people who say this is a book of fairy tales, myths, and that the further back you go the less real and definite are the people — shadowy, as if Abraham was a name for a tribe wandering around. It wasn't — Abraham was a man. So was Enoch, so was Noah. Those who doubt the existence of these men are going to get an awful shock when they meet them. "Well, Noah, I thought you were just a fairy tale." What a shock! Let us look at them. They are in historical order; they are all in one pedigree line. A marvellous pedigree of faith goes down this line. It is not a pedigree of flesh alone because there were others in that pedigree who did not survive and are not on God's honours list. The pedigree in your life that is most important is not your pedigree of flesh, but of faith.

"By faith, Abel...." What did he do? Well, he had the right attitude towards God. When he and his brother Cain came and offered things to God, God said "no" to Cain and "yes" to Abel. Why? Some people have said because Abel's offering was an offering of animals, which included blood, which was acceptable to God, and Cain's was an offering of fruits and vegetables, which didn't have blood in them and therefore wasn't acceptable — that is a possible explanation, though I don't think there's any scriptural ground for saying it. They were each bringing what they had raised. Cain looked after the soil, while Abel looked after the animals. It would be grossly unfair if God therefore refused Cain just because he brought the only thing he could bring. I don't think that's the real answer. We are told one hint in scripture that points to the real answer — that God looked not at the offering but at the attitude of the offerer. In Cain's heart, he did not find faith and in Abel's heart he did. Which means you can go through the same religious ritual and rigmarole and one can do it in faith and one can do it without faith. One of the lovely things that happens when you come to have faith is that rigmarole and ritual and the rest of it can come alive. Things you said like a parrot for years suddenly mean something. Why? Because there is faith now in the attitude.

I was talking to one lady and I tried to convince her that if she believed in Jesus, one day she would have a new body. She was crippled with rheumatoid arthritis and I was trying to encourage her. She said, "Well, I've never heard such a thing before."

"You go to church?" I asked.

"Yes," she replied, "I go to my parish church every Sunday."

I said, "You've said this in church every Sunday."

"When have I said that?"

"Well, you've said, 'I believe in the resurrection of the body.'"

"Oh, that."

Oh that! By faith you can bring an offering to the Lord but is there faith in it? Are you bringing it because you are staking your whole future on the God to whom you are offering that gift?

So Abel had the faith and Cain did not. Cain was jealous and God warned him that sin was prowling around the door of his heart and would leap in if he gave it a chance. God was saying: Cain, get your attitude right, get your heart right, get even your face right. There was a wrong look on your face when you came to worship. Get that right and then I'll accept your offering.

But Cain didn't, he went out and killed Abel. But you know, death is never the last word in the life of a righteous man. Abel is among those who are still alive, even though his blood was shed by his own brother, the first murderer of history.

Now let us move on to Enoch. I love the account of Enoch — the man who never died because he pleased God; the man who went for a walk one day and just walked right into glory, never came back. What a way to go—marvellous! Why did Enoch walk with God? Because he believed in God. Notice that it doesn't just say he *lived for* God, it is something much more intimate, he *walked with* God. That implies a deep personal relationship, a daily walk, step by step. Every step he took — he never took it alone, he was always stepping with God. No wonder God gave him the inestimable privilege of never tasting death. Elijah was the only other one to have that same experience. Enoch stands there as one who believed in God's existence, as one who believed that God was interested in him, as one who knew God and walked with him.

Now we move on to Noah. He had an announcement given to him of something unprecedented, unimaginable. He began to build a ship in the middle of a desert. No wonder the people laughed and mocked. No wonder it has been a subject of humour ever since. Noah was the man who believed that when God said a thing it would happen, that was it and nothing could stop it. He just went on building the ark. It is a very profound situation because in fact Noah brought judgment on everybody else. When one man in a company of people believes and others do not share his faith then that brings judgment on all the rest — it shows them up; it reveals them as unbelievers. There only needs to be one believer in a whole family and the rest of the family is condemned because they have got every opportunity, there is in their presence someone who believes in the invisible, to whom the future is as real as the past. When that happens then everybody else is in the wrong. Faith puts a man in the right and everybody else in connection with that man in the wrong. That was what happened in Noah's day. Only seven other people shared his faith — his wife, his three sons and their wives. Eight souls out of an entire society, in an area where there just hadn't been rain and floods, and yet he went

149

on building the ark—Noah the man of faith.

Do you believe in judgment to come? Do you believe that Jesus has said that what happened in Noah's day is going to be repeated once more, and that as it was in the days of Noah, so it shall be in the days of the coming of the Son of Man? Mind you, the physical element which will dissolve the world will be different. It was water; it will be fire this time. But do you *believe* it? Are you as certain of it as Noah was? Just think of the implications for your life if you were as sure of the second great catastrophe as Noah was sure of the first. Think of the concern you would have for your family, your sons and daughters-in-law. Think of the concern you would have for your neighbours. Noah put himself in the right, he was accounted righteous, but he put everybody else in the wrong, unless they shared his faith.

Now we come to the greatest man of faith of all, the greatest believer in the Old Testament — and it is never too late, this man believed at the age of eighty. It is hard to understand just how much his faith cost him until you look at the photographs of the excavations at Ur of the Chaldees, which is where he lived for the first eighty years of his life. They had modern fireplaces, they had running water, they had central heating in their homes—it is a marvellous place. The ruins tell us what a magnificent civilization it was, what comforts there were, what sophistication. Abraham, at eighty years of age, believed that there was another country that was better. For the rest of his life he lived in a tent. He never had a place to call his own. He finally had one little piece of property, one cave in which to bury his wife, and that was all.

At his advanced age he set off on a journey that was to take him hundreds of miles through alluvial plain, through desert, through mountain — and all the while he was looking for another country. His obedience showed his faith. The fact is that when he got to the country that God showed him he still did not build a house, he still didn't say, "Well, must get some central heating in." He still lived in a tent and he still said, "I'm a stranger and a sojourner. I'm not going to build a house because I know that God is going to build a city, and anything less than that would be imperfect, so I'm just not going to build." So he didn't.

Consider the greatest example of faith. One day he was sitting outside his tent door looking up at the stars, and he was a lonely old man. There was one huge disappointment. He had got a very beautiful wife but she seemed to lack something—she had never conceived. It was all the greater disappointment because they had been such a fruitful family. Sarah was barren. The line comes to an end. Everything might have finished with Abraham, but when you get to the end of human resources you are at the beginning of the resources of God. When human beings would draw the line, God breaks through it.

"Abraham."

And he looked up at the stars. "Yes, Lord?"

"You're going to have a baby."

"What me?"

"Yes. You see those stars, Abraham? Your descendants will be as many as the stars."

Amazing, isn't it, that the naked eye in those days could only see as many as six thousand stars but the Bible says, "Your descendants will be as many as the stars and the grains of sand on the seashore." Well now, surely there could be no comparison between those two numbers. Six thousand stars? Why, you could almost hold six thousand grains of sand in two hands but God knew what he was talking about, and now science knows that there are not just six thousand stars, there are far more. It came true and God was as good as his word.

Now all these, says Hebrews, were looking for a better

country —which they didn't receive but in which they did believe. Isn't it marvellous to receive something by believing? You may not receive the title deeds, you may have no tangible proof to show anyone else, but you have received by believing. They did not receive the country, but they died in faith. What a test of faith: to get right through your life and never have what you have been promised, and to die believing that you were going to get it — the sort of tremendous faith a dying thief on a cross showed when he said, "Lord, remember me when you come into your kingdom."

To go all your life without receiving the blessing of God and to know that that blessing is certain is a bigger faith than faith in the blessings we do receive. They died in faith simply taking God at his word. Their eyes looked beyond the land of Canaan to a better country. So don't think of the Jews as people who look to an earthly promised land. These great men of faith realised that even Canaan on earth was simply a foretaste, a shadow, the substance of which was elsewhere. Abraham looked for the city and the country. Therefore, they remained strangers, aliens, pilgrims even in the land of promise, and this is what we are today.

Peter, writing a letter much later, said, "We are aliens and strangers...." That is why God is not ashamed to link his name with those who believe. Who is God? He is the God of Abraham, Isaac and Jacob. He is not ashamed to be called that. Abraham had his faults, of course. The Bible is an honest book. It tells you the faults of Abraham, Isaac and Jacob. Abraham tried to pass his wife off as his sister because he was scared that he would be killed in order that Pharaoh might have her. It was a dastardly deed—he was willing to let his wife go and become part of the harem of Pharaoh to save his own skin. What a thing to do to your own wife! Yet God is not ashamed to be named by Abraham

because Abraham believed, and that means he is not ashamed
to be named by you.

We move to the second half of the list—patriarchs and
prophets. We return to Abraham although we just ended
with him, but Abraham seems to be the watershed. He is the
beginning and the end of faith in the Old Testament. There
is another remarkable example of Abraham's faith. The little
boy Isaac was born — his name meaning "laughter" because
both Abraham and Sarah had laughed at the possibility. They
called the boy "Joke", that is what the name means. What
a joke it was in their old age. So little "Joke" came into the
world and they loved that happy little boy. Then God said,
"Abraham, kill him." Abraham set off with the wood for
his own son's execution. What a moment, looking up into
his dad's face and saying, "Dad, we've got the wood and
the knife and everything, but what are you going to kill?"

What a moment. "The Lord will provide, son."

Then the horrible moment, Abraham must have had to
look away as he tied the boy. How could he look into the his
eyes? He tied him, laid him on the altar and got the knife.
He was going to end God's promise, but how could he bring
himself to do it? For two reasons. First, he believed that
if God had promised something he would do it. Therefore,
secondly, having thought it through—how could God do
this if he has told me to kill my son? It must be because
God intends to raise him from the dead.... It was the
only conclusion he could come to. But it shows that he
believed that God could raise the dead. Abraham believed
in resurrection power.

There is remarkably little faith in resurrection in the Old
Testament if you search the pages, but Abraham stands out
as believing in the resurrection. Believing God could raise
the dead; he was prepared to kill his own son because he
believed that God could raise him from the dead—what faith!

That is why when he left the servants, before going the last bit of the journey to Mount Moriah, he turned to them and said, "You wait here and we will return." Did you ever notice that little "we"? He was not trying to fool the servants and cover up, he is expressing faith. So it is natural that Isaac, when he grew up, shared that faith with such a dad.

How did Isaac show his faith? In a very quiet way, in not nearly as spectacular a way. Isaac showed his faith when he came to die. He made a will and testament, and he left to his son the property that he had never had. It is as if I made my will and went to a lawyer and said to him, "I want to leave my son Buckingham Palace." Can you imagine what the lawyer would say?

But when Isaac came to make his will he just made it very simply by word of mouth. He said, "I leave this land to you." How could he? It wasn't his but he believed. Jacob did the same thing. The old man, leaning on his staff, says to his twelve sons, "I leave you this land, and I leave you that, and I leave you the other," and none of it was his to leave. Remarkable, isn't it? What faith these men had.

So the record continues: Joseph, son of Jacob — look at his faith when he came to die. He was down in Egypt and so were all the people of Israel and they were going to be there three or four hundred years, but Joseph said, "When I'm dead, keep my bones in a pot, and when you get out of here and go to that promised land take my bones with you." When they set off from Egypt they took with them a coffin. The last word in the book of Genesis is the word "coffin". They took the coffin and the remains of Joseph, and they carried it for forty years through the wilderness and got it in to the promised land. But he had faith: "Take me there with you, I believe you'll go."

Moses—a supreme figure, perhaps, of Jewish history. His faith showed first in his parents' faith. They saw this boy and they said, "He's extraordinary, we must keep him." They put him in the river Nile, that's where all the other boys were being thrown. They were being killed by being thrown to the crocodiles by the Egyptian overlords, but they took their boy and they put him in a floating basket, and by faith they waited to see what God would do, and Pharaoh's daughter came to bathe.

He grew up — and a young man's faith is tested when he has a choice. Shall I share my parents' faith or shall I enjoy the pleasures of sin? At forty years of age Moses made the made the right choice and chose to suffer mistreatment with the people of God rather than to enjoy the pleasures of sin for a season.

It takes faith for a young man to do that, to be a Jacob and not an Esau. Why did Jacob get the inheritance? We think it is so unfair that he played a dirty trick on Esau, don't we? But Jacob knew his brother Esau. Jacob knew that Esau would rather have a bowl of soup now than some vague inheritance in the future. Jacob was so sure of that inheritance, even though his father hadn't got it to give. Jacob had the faith, and that was why he got it. Not because he played a dirty trick, not because he was clever, but because he had faith to believe that he would inherit something his father couldn't give him. Esau didn't believe that, so he said, "I'll have a bowl of soup now because that's tangible, that's something I can see, and I need it and I would like to have that."

Can you see the line of faith? Moses got them out of Egypt. The desert was behind them, the mountains on their right, the Egyptian army on their left, the Red Sea in front. Moses was told, "Speak to the people of Israel that they go forward," and forward they went in faith. As soon as they did, the Red Sea dried up and they walked through on dry ground. It was faith, not a coincidence. As soon as people without faith stepped in they were drowned.

We move on on to Jericho. You may have seen the remains dug out by archeologists—what walls! They had no battering rams, no engines of war to tackle such walls, and this was the first city they came to. They marched around it, shouted "Hallelujah" and down the walls came —by faith. One stretch of wall would not have broken down because there were two walls and because the city was limited by the walls it was overcrowded and they had built houses on the walls. They have discovered the rafters across the two walls on which the houses were built, so there were windows looking down over the steep outside wall. In one of those houses lived a prostitute. She saw the Jews without any battering rams, but she believed they would get the city. She believed that God would give them her city. So when the men came sneaking into the city she was on the lookout, she was out on the corner. She saw them, she invited them in, hid them and said, "I know that God is going to give you this city." They said, "Hang a scarlet thread out of the window and then we'll know which is your house, and you will be safe." Rahab became an ancestress of our Lord. She is in our Lord's family tree, and Rahab became part of the people of God. Because she was a prostitute? No, but because she was a believing prostitute, that's why — because she had faith.

God doesn't ask for perfection, he doesn't ask for moral purity to start with. That is his object and end, but he doesn't ask for it to begin with. If he did, we would never make it. The biggest mistake the Pharisees ever made was to think that you have got to start with that before you can be right with God. But it is the man who cries, "God be merciful to me, a sinner" who goes down to his house justified, right in God's sight —in God's good books. Rahab is one of the heroes of faith. She is only one of two women mentioned in this chapter—Sarah and Rahab. I wonder how Sarah would feel about being linked with Rahab. But to God she's one of God's heroines of history — she believed.

Gideon, Samson, Barak, Jephthah, David, Samuel, the prophets. It is a very long line of witnesses. Consider Gideon fighting the Midianites and others with only three hundred men. We have a list of people who right from the time of the entry into the promised land until the time of the first kings fought against overwhelming odds and stayed in that land—a historical period which is repeating itself in our own day and which we can see in our newspapers.

I was reminded of all this in 1948 when six million Arabs swore to push less than one million Jews into the Mediterranean and wipe out this people who had come to stake a claim in the Middle East. But no, God is with his people. Through faith they subdued kingdoms, they became valiant in war, they became conquerors. Daniel conquered the lions. Shadrach, Meshach, and Abednego conquered the fury of flames. Elijah and Elisha both escaped assassination. Women received their dead — Elijah brought back to life a widow's son.

But now comes an even more startling development and it is thrilling. Some conquered by faith, and some were conquered and still showed faith. Some escaped the edge of the sword by faith. Some were put to the sword by faith. Some were raised from the dead by faith. Some were sawn in two by faith. The Bible can see both as examples of faith, and until we have seen that we have not seen the full picture. It is so natural and instinctive for us to think that it is by faith that we get out of trouble. But sometimes it is by faith that we go into it and face it. It is by faith that we can be saved from death, and by faith that we can die. This is the astonishing truth that is coming through now. When we realise this then we can glorify God in our bodies —whatever happens. We may be healed, and we can glorify God for the faith to be healed. We may not be healed, and we can still glorify God by the faith that we have in him. We can glorify God by becoming martyrs as well as by being saved from death.

By faith we subdue and by faith we succumb, but it can be by faith both ways. So these great heroines of faith and heroes of faith did wonderful things, and horrible things were done to them. They wandered around in sheepskins and goatskins. They hid in caves and holes in the ground, and that is going to happen again. There will be a time when God's people have to leave the urban areas and get into the wilderness. In the reign of Antichrist, that is certain to come. We shall be out in the country. We won't be able to buy and sell in the shops unless we have branded on us the national insurance number of the world dictator.

Horrible things have happened and will happen to God's people. But the truth is this: though the world considers them not worthy to live in the world, the world is not worthy of them. Think of this passage when you see Christians separated out because they are Christians, shunned because they are Christians, ostracised because they are Christians — when you suffer just a little social ostracism at work because you are a Christian, because you are different, let me tell you that this epistle is saying clearly and forcefully that the world is not worthy of you. It is not that you are not worthy to mix with them. It is a judgment on those who persecute.

All these witnesses are waiting. They have not received the promises. They are still waiting for the better country. Why? Because they are waiting for a better community. It is the community that makes the country; the people who make the place. What turns your house into a home? The fact that the family is there. The witnesses are being kept waiting until you and I join them. Isn't that exciting?

Abraham is waiting for David Pawson to join him so that the blessing can come. Doesn't that thrill you? Well it thrills me. Put your own name in it, it will thrill you. Isaac is waiting, Rahab is waiting and Joshua is waiting. They are waiting for us and longing for the day when we join them and we all receive our resurrection bodies. Old Testament and New Testament become one testament, one last will and testament of Jesus Christ, and there shall be one flock and one Shepherd—that's the truth.

We shall all be made perfect *together*. I am certain of that. Therefore, with this cloud of witnesses around us.... The emphasis is on witnesses to the Lord, testifiers: one after another they come into the witness box and testify. With such a cloud of witnesses the case is complete.

Let us therefore strip off everything that handicaps—it may be something that is good but we could run better without it. An athlete doesn't put on gumboots and a duffel coat to win a race, good though these may be in themselves. Let us strip off every weight, anything that would hold us back, even if it is good. Let us strip off everything that is bad. We are called to strip off *some* things that are good and *all* things that are bad.

We are not to look at Abraham or Isaac or Jacob — we are not to pray to these men. We are to fix our gaze on one—the pioneer and perfecter of our faith who went through it all, who died, who faced it all, who himself died without having received the promises, but who for the joy that was set before him endured the cross, despising the shame. He said, "Father, into thy hands I commit my spirit." He was exercising the same faith as all these witnesses but to a superlative degree. His faith was tested in that darkness to the limit, "My God, my God, why have you deserted me?" But it came through triumphant, "It's finished, Father." So he is the pioneer, he begins our faith. He pioneered its pattern. He has shown us how to believe, and he is the perfecter of our faith. He fired the pistol to set you running, and he is there holding the tape at the winning post, so fix your eyes on Jesus Christ.

In a church where I ministered we have a tapestry, most beautifully embroidered by three Roman Catholic nuns. One of them, just filled with the Holy Spirit of the risen Jesus, was given visions, pictures in her mind of the glory of the Lord. She then translated them as best she could to two others who got busy with a needle and thread and translated the vision in materials. Every stitch is full of faith. In the one we borrowed to hang up, there is a great cloud of witnesses, yet they are secondary. Your eye is drawn away from them and above them to the glory of the cross, which was not a black, dead cross. It was full of glory, a light, alive because Christ is alive. That had to happen first—he endured the cross, despised the shame. But what faith he had to go through it and say, "Into your hands I commit my spirit." His faith was honoured and he is now in that better country as our high priest. He is now making our faith better still. We, with this great cloud of witnesses, are looking to him — running our race until one day we will be made perfect.

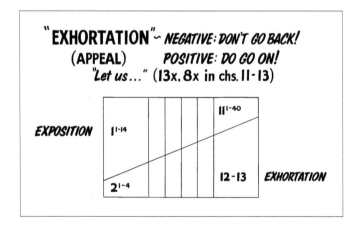

9

FAITH'S PIONEER AND PERFECTER
Read 12:1 – 17

A. PERSEVERANCE (1)
1. Stripped
    a. Some good things b. All bad things
2. Stretched
B. PATTERN (2a)
1. Pioneer
    a. Trail-blazer b. Starter
2. Perfecter
    a. Leader b. Finisher
C. PERSECUTION (2b–3)
1. Consider himself
2. Compare yourself
D. PUNISHMENT (4–17)
1. Hardship (4–13)
2. Holiness (14–17)

Now we are no longer looking *back* into the Old Testament at the figures of history, at the tabernacle, the sacrifices, and all the rest that went through those centuries. We are now looking *up* and we see Abraham, Moses, Elijah, and we see a great cloud of witnesses. Above all, we see in the middle of them the one who fixes our gaze upon him — Jesus, and we look to him. We are leaving behind the comparisons between the Old and the New Testament and turning away from the visible to the invisible, which we can see by faith. We are turning away from the copies to the real, from the earthly to the heavenly and we are getting our sights fixed, and how important it is to do that. Sometimes life seems to me like going through a jungle, and you lose your way through the week. From Monday to Saturday you seem to be so immersed in the undergrowth of everyday life —tangled up.

We look now at this cloud of witnesses. It is no accident that many interpreters of Hebrews chapter 12 have got the impression that the writer is thinking of a gigantic stadium. Since it was almost certainly written to the Christians in Rome, you could understand that, because Rome was full of these big sports stadia. I have looked at some of the ruins of them and have never seen such big sports fields, particularly the one where Caligula's palace overlooked the sports field so that he could lie in bed and from his balcony watch the games—gigantic arenas with great, big serried ranks of grandstands. Go into the Roman Collosseum, find the building there that will hold seven thousand people, with a separate entrance and staircase to every block of seats—it is a marvellous construction. There in that place you just have row upon row of spectators looking down. Some have felt that Hebrews 12 is saying, "Since we are surrounded by such a great cloud of spectators, let us run the race." In other words: "Let the crowd spur you on." If that is the right interpretation we may take from this that Abraham, Moses and Elijah are watching us. Those who ran well in their day are looking down to see how we run, saying, "I wonder if he'll make it. Come on, come on!"

That is the impression that many have got from the verse, and I would not like to do anything to spoil that impression because the communion of saints is a very real item in the Christian's experience, the knowledge that we are linked with those in heaven. We know that they are as close to

Christ, if not closer than we are. Therefore, if we hold one hand of Christ he holds them with the other. We feel the communion of saints, we know that we are surrounded by a great cloud of witnesses, and with angels and archangels we worship the Lord of glory. But I am not sure that that is the real meaning of the word "witnesses". It implies that they are witnessing what *we* do. But the word would never have that meaning anywhere else. Let me tell you what I think it means. It does not mean spectators. It means those who themselves, whose own lives, give testimony to what faith in the invisible can do. It is more a word taken from the courtroom than the sports stadium. It is as if you have sat in a gigantic court and witness after witness has stood in the box and said, "I believed". That is the real meaning of the word: not witnesses of us, but *witnesses to him*. In other words, we are not the first to have run this race.

When Christians get into problems, we invariably think we are the first to have such problems, and that is our problem until we find out we are not. Believe me, there is nothing you experience as a Christian that is new. We are not the first to have run; we are surrounded by a great cloud of witnesses. Read the Bible carefully, you will find there all the problems you have in your spiritual life. You will find that they had them. The Bible is honest, it does not try to paint plaster saints who had a wonderful life and were never depressed, never had a dark night of the soul. David is utterly honest, "Why are you cast down, O my soul?" So there is nothing new.

The inspiration the cloud of witnesses is to us is not so much that they are watching us, but that they are witnesses to him. That they have been along the course before, and that they had faith, and they believed, and they endured as seeing him who is invisible, and they got there. This is what puts heart into us, that we are just one of a long line of testimony to what faith can be and do. That, I think, is the real meaning. It is a witness to their faith, not so much to ours.

This is a very practical passage. We began by looking at the prophets, then the angels, then the apostles of the Old Testament—Moses and Joshua, then the priests, then the tabernacle, then the sacrifices, then the great heroes of faith. We have gone up and up. Now we have reached the top. What do we do about it? Sit down? No, "Let us run...." In a sense, once you have reached the top it is a little easier to run, but still an effort; it still requires discipline. There is a race to be run, which now we are going to think about.

It is absolutely vital in the Christian life, if you are going to run the race, that you get your eyes off other people and onto Jesus—that sounds such a simple thing. You would think after all that has been written in Hebrews about Abraham, Moses and the rest of them it would say "fix your eyes on them and do what they did" —but that would be fatal. One of the mistakes that many young Christians make, and some older ones, is to look at other Christians to measure their own experience by what other people experience, to try to imitate others. I don't know how many Christians I have met who read the life of George Muller and rushed off to start an orphanage, and many of them came unstuck.

You see, you have got to look to Jesus, and if he tells you to do something about orphans, then do it. It is fatal to read an account of what another saint has done and say, "Right, I'm going to run that race. I'm going to beat him" or, "I'm going to do what he did." No, after all the heroes of chapter eleven, forget the cloud of witnesses now, and look to Jesus. There are two reasons why you should do this and not fix your eyes on all these heroes of faith. One is that they didn't get there; not one of them. It says at the end of Hebrews 11 all of them failed to receive the promise. Why? Because God is holding them until they can be made perfect with us. They have not got there yet, they have not arrived yet, so don't copy them or you won't get there.

The second reason is that it says, "Let us run the course that God has marked out for us." I find great encouragement in that. He has not called me to be an Abraham or a Moses. He only called Abraham to be an Abraham and Moses to be a Moses. Isn't that encouraging? He has marked out a course for me, and he is asking me to run the course marked out for me. He is not asking me to run anybody else's race for them. That's why the Bible constantly says, "Mind your own business" — in various words of course. Peter said to Jesus after the resurrection, "Now what about John? What's your future plan for him?" And Jesus virtually said, "Mind your own business." He said, "What is that to you? Follow me."

So let us look at Jesus and run the race marked out for us. Let us see that we get there. You may be called upon to be a martyr or you may not. You may be called on to look after orphans — or not. The important thing is that we run the race that has been set for us. So the saints cannot help us directly—that is why we should not pray to them. Look to Jesus, go to him. Ask him for your course and for the grace to run it.

We need to *persevere* to run the race. We need to remove everything that hinders us. We have noticed that good things may have to be discarded if you are going to run the race, not just bad things. This will be different things for different people—to a rich young ruler Jesus said, "You'd better cut out your bank balance." He doesn't say that to everybody, but he marked out the course for that man. You can't run a race if you are overweight. Physical overweight can be a spiritual handicap, which is why Christians have always included gluttony among the deadly sins. It is mentioned more than we care to realise in the book of Proverbs. But there is such a thing as emotional overweight or intellectual overweight. An athlete is an ascetic—you can't both be an athlete and live the high life at the same time. So let us run the race with perseverance and get rid of anything good that could hold us back and hinder our running. Then, it goes without saying, get rid of all the bad things too—some of the good things and all the bad things.

We talk about "besetting sin" as if it means "our one failing" but it doesn't mean that here. It means sin general. It is not "our besetting sin" but "the sin which besets us" and that is not one thing. It really means "Don't run through clay." Have you ever tried to run through wet clay? I have done so on a farm in boots, and it is not long before you're up to your knees, weighted down with the stuff. The faster you run, the more you pick up, it seems.

Strip off whatever tends to cling, whatever tends to stick, to pull you down, to hold you where you are—that is what it is saying here — a very vivid thought. Notice that it assumes that you know *what* mud clings. It assumes too that it will be an *effort* to run, that you will have to prepare yourself and discipline yourself. It means, thirdly, that you are *able* to strip it off. The Bible never tells you to do anything that you cannot do by the grace of God. If you don't strip for this race, what will happen to you? Verse 12 tells you: "Drooping arms, shaky knees, and lame limbs" —and you will not be able to run.

The thing we need to do is to *stretch*. Have you ever watched an athlete straining every muscle to go forward? Consider what Paul wrote: "Forgetting the things that are behind...." That is the stripping part — and stretching forward, straining forward to the things that are before: "I press on towards the goal". In other words, you are an athlete as a Christian, and you are not a good athlete unless you stretch forward, unless you have the goal in mind all the time.

The letter to the Hebrews again and again, as we have seen, is saying this: It is not whether you have started the Christian life that is so important, it is whether you are continuing and whether you are determined to complete, so that when you get to your dying day you can say with the apostle Paul, "I have kept the faith, I have finished the course". That means his course, which was for so many years, and he knew that if he died now he had finished the course and he had arrived. Our Lord Jesus had said, "It is finished." To finish your course—Jesus finished it in thirty-three years; Paul probably finished it in fifty years. It is not the length of life. It is not, "I've lived a long, full life." That is not finishing the course; it is completing what God gave you to do, and this involves perseverance.

There are many Christians who set off but don't arrive. There are many believers who got soundly converted, but who could not say when they died, "I have finished the course." They died halfway along or even a third of the way along. Like the many who died in the wilderness after leaving Egypt and never saw the promised land. Out of two and a half million people who left Egypt and were redeemed by God, only two entered the promised land.

What did Paul say just before that? "I do not count myself yet to have arrived". A Christian is not someone who has arrived, and should never give the impression to others: I have arrived now that I am a Christian. The truth is that when I become a Christian I have not arrived at anything. I have started right, that is all. For the first time in my life I am now living on course, in the right direction. How important it is then not to neglect passages like Hebrews 6 and 10 which warn us what can happen to those who drift, to those who neglect so great a salvation, to those who don't press on, who don't keep the goal clearly in mind.

If you are going have a goal you have got to look at it.

Jesus said something about putting your hand to the plough and looking back. And when Peter tried walking on the water, as long as he looked at Jesus he was fine, but as soon as he took his eyes off Jesus, he was lost. I remember hearing a story about a young boy learning to plough, and having ploughed with a couple of horses in front of me up and down the field, I can say it is a most satisfying thing. But if once you start looking at your work, thinking, "My that's a good furrow," then it is hopeless.

A young man learning to plough was told by the farmer when he had gone across the field the first time, "Fix your eyes on something at the far end of the field." He did, and it finished just as bad. The farmer said, "What on earth were you looking at?" He replied, "Well, I fixed my eyes on a cow in the next field." That is what it is to fix your eyes on a saint, incidentally. There is only one goal and you need to fix your eyes on Jesus because he is the only one who ran and won. He is the one who reached the finishing tape by the age of thirty-three, and by his grace we can do the same. Looking not sideways or backwards but forward, you keep in a straight line and you go straight for your goal.

Two titles are given to Jesus here which both have a double meaning. Again, the commentators are so divided about this and I am going to keep everybody happy by saying that both meanings are right so we need not argue about which it is. First, he is the *pioneer* of our faith—and that has a double meaning. Second, he is the *perfecter* of our faith and that has a double meaning too. "Pioneer" can mean "a trailblazer", someone who has gone first and marked out the course. Certainly Jesus has done this for us. He has been through it all. But the other meaning of the word "pioneer" is "originator"—the one who said, "Go", the one who started you off. Which meaning is it? I am sure it is a bit of both. Jesus is not only the one who ran the course first and was the trailblazer, the pioneer marking out the course, but he then fired the pistol that set me going on the course. He was the one who started me off, who gave me faith, who started my Christian life.

"Perfecter" means somebody who got to the end of the course, somebody who had a perfect faith. It also means someone who will finish my course for me and someone who will perfect my faith. The word "our" is not in the original. It is "the pioneer and perfecter of faith," but in the second meaning of each of those words we can legitimately put in the word "our" — the pioneer and perfecter of *our* faith. He sets me going and he is at the winning post waiting for me and saying, "Come on." He is calling us to keep going until we feel the tape on our chest and we are through and can say, "We finished the course." So he is the pioneer, our example and our coach. We are to fix our vision on him, which means, of course, seeing invisible things.

We have thought, firstly, about the *perseverance* with which we run, secondly about the *pattern* to whom we look, Jesus himself. Thirdly, I want you to realise that the race includes *persecution*. If you look at Jesus you will see this. He ran the race, he finished the course and what happened to him? He was crucified. For him the course led through Calvary. He longed to find a way around this course. But this course led through this great obstacle and instead of running round it, he ran right through it. His course led to Calvary. He was despised and rejected of men and suffered opposition from sinful men.

It is a shock to realise when you start running this race that there are many other people who don't want you to run it, and that there will be opposition from sinful men who don't run the race themselves — they are not even in it and don't want to be. As soon as you start running the race, those people at your workplace who are not in the race themselves will try to stop you running it. It is a sad fact that for Christianity there is always a cross; there is always going to be opposition, shame and humiliation. Remember that Jesus was a very sensitive man. Remember that the worst part of crucifixion, humanly speaking, was not the pain but the humiliation. Strung up stark naked in front of everybody's gaze—it is a horrible thing.

Do you know what it says here? "He despised that he was being despised." What a phrase! When you can say, "I despise being despised," you have won the race. Because it is not easy to be laughed at and it is not easy to feel you are different. It is not easy to be humiliated, to look undignified, but every Christian will. We look silly to the world, we look crazy. Consider Jesus. Persecution will come, but consider him "who endured the cross, despising the shame." How was he able to go through with it? The answer is very simple— because he kept his eyes on the future rather than the present. Even if the present was humiliating, the future was glory. Even if the present was painful, the future was joy. Even if the present was unhappiness, the future was happiness — for the joy set before him....

This indeed is the great secret of surviving the tough patches in the Christian life, overcoming the hurdles and obstacles of the race. Overcoming the opposition—going on running when the crowd is shouting not, "Come on" but, "Stop, go back!" You go on running for the joy set before you. Not the joy you may be *experiencing at the moment*— you may not be, but *the joy set before you.* Oh, the world will laugh at you. They will say, "Pie in the sky when you die." They will say, "You're just deluding yourself," but you have got to keep your eyes fixed on the invisible, on Jesus who lives now, and the heaven that exists — and for the joy set before you, run. So there is a second thing you need to do when considering persecution. *Consider him and compare your own sufferings to his*. Have you resisted to blood yet? No. Have we had to be crucified yet? No. Have they done anything approaching crucifixion to you at the office? No. Then don't grow faint, don't become weary. You see, if when you are going through a bit of unpopularity, some social ostracism, you just consider him and compare yourself to him, then frankly you will keep going.

What we have to face is infinitesimal compared with what he went through. What we go through now is small compared with the eternal weight of glory that will be revealed. You see the thing in perspective. We go down and get depressed when we lose sight of Jesus and we lose sight of heaven, and the present sufferings become magnified, self-pity sets in and depression follows. Then we have lost sight of the future and the invisible and we are going downhill.

Look what Jesus went through — and where is he now? He is sitting on a throne. Look, we are going to sit on thrones with him, he promised that to those who overcome. So if you are looking for a crown, can't you go through a little more suffering? Of course you can. You have not been through what he went through. You remember Corrie Ten Boom's *The Hiding Place*? How she and her sister Betsy were stripped naked and stood in front of German soldiers in the concentration camp and the German soldiers commented on their aging figures and laughed at them. It was humiliating— what a thing for a woman to go through at that age. But how did she get through it? It was Betsy who said, "They stripped Jesus and they laughed at him," and they came through it. They got their eyes fixed on Jesus and on the future. They knew that their days would not end in a concentration camp but in the glory of heaven, alongside Jesus who went through what they were going through. That is how you run the race: you keep your eyes fixed ahead.

Now I want you to face one final fact: the Christian life

is full of trouble. Never believe those who say, "Come to Christ and your troubles are over." It is a lie of the devil and Jesus didn't say it. He was too honest for that. He said, "In the world you will have tribulation" — and tribulation means big trouble. "But be of good cheer, I have overcome the world." The fourth fact of the race is this, and it is a very hard one to accept at first: *If you become a Christian, you will suffer more than you did before.* The reason is very simple: because you now have a heavenly Father who chastises you. Any trouble that comes to you is allowed by him, and therefore it comes from him.

This is a sobering thought, but the Christian, when he gets into a tough time, should ask the question: What is my heavenly Father trying to teach me? What is he trying to say to me? He allowed this to come. Why is he chastising me? It is a very important question to ask because trouble does come from God. If it didn't, then get worried. If God never troubles you, then, says this letter, you should ask whether you are an illegitimate child, calling yourself a son of God but with no legal rights to do so—a very stern thing to say.

Let us just look at it for a moment. What does it mean? I think we have got to rethink fatherhood. This may be a sweeping statement, but I think there is evidence enough in our law courts to support it. On the whole the fathers of Britain are not good disciplinarians. I believe we are therefore storing up a terrible harvest to reap. I have sat in a court and heard a father of a nine-year old boy say, "I can do nothing with him." The reason why he said that when the boy was nine, I believe, is that he did nothing with him when he was five. I know that in many homes the mother is left to discipline the children. The father abdicates that responsibility, maybe doesn't even see enough of the kids to do it. Therefore, projecting our own image into heaven, we create God in our own image and we have then got a God who is a grandfather. You know what a grandfather is? He has all the joy of children but none of the responsibilities, and can go back home after a few days when he has had enough. So we have got this grandfather picture of God and it comes out again and again because people cannot accept that God is a God who punishes. You can see why they accept this false view, because they are reading their own kind of fatherhood into God's. But God's fatherhood is true fatherhood, and true fatherhood disciplines. If it doesn't, what a harvest you will reap later!

Now remember this was written to Rome. Have you ever heard of *patria potestas*? That means fatherly discipline. In the early days of the Roman republic, family life was strong and fatherhood was strong. There is hardly any trace of divorce in the Roman republic. It was when it became an empire, and when the emperor himself began to drift, that family life began to break up and divorce and remarriage became frequent. A father was given by law absolute rights over his son. In fact, when a son was born the father could keep him or discard him and no law would touch him. He had the right to bind or scourge his son. He had the right to sell his son as a slave or even execute him.

Now a good Roman father who exercised discipline produced a good son. Of course, the absolute authority of a Roman father could be terribly abused and was. But in the early days of the republic, a Roman father was reckoned to be totally responsible for his son and that applied until your father died. If you were sixty years of age and your father was eighty-five it still applied. It is against this background that the writer to these Christians in Rome said: You have had earthly fathers who disciplined you. It was painful. All discipline is painful.

If you come to Christ, you have now got a heavenly Father and discipline is going to be painful. Of course it is, you thank God for it because if you didn't have it you could question whether you were a son at all. But we can also say this: that a father has a purpose in discipline if he is a good father. A bad father, of course, will abuse his authority and will simply punish the child to work off his own feelings of frustration and anger. But a good father does it for one reason —he wants his son to grow up to be a gentleman. A good father looks to the future, not the present. He is prepared to cause a painful present that there might be a lovely future, and woe betide us if we neglect this truth.

"Endure hardship," says the letter to the Hebrews. It is going to be tough; endure it because God is allowing it. Why? Because it is his plan for your life—the course he has marked out for you is this: holiness in this life, happiness in the next. The world simply wants to reverse that and says, "Surely God wants me to be happy here, and he can make me holy hereafter." That is the total opposite of God's will. God loves us so he is prepared to cause us pain if it will help us to get holy. What love you have got to have to do that.

So this is the truth that we must remember as we run the race. Psalm 119, the longest psalm in the Bible, is a perfect illustration and full of wonderful truths. Here is a marvellous one from v. 67f., "Before I was afflicted I went astray, but now I observe your word. It is good for me that I have been afflicted that I may learn your statutes." There is something strong about that verse, isn't there? This is no weak namby-pamby Christian riding on a sofa to heaven; this is no easy path. This is somebody running the race; this is somebody who has his eyes fixed on the goal.

A very practical final appeal: therefore strengthen your feeble arms and your weak knees. Make level paths for your feet, so that the lame may not be disabled, but rather be healed. In other words, in a simple word: no stragglers. We realise that we are not running as individuals but as a body — we are running together, and the way I run is going to affect the way somebody else runs. It is more like a cross-country run with a group of us running, and one person can poison the race. How? First of all we are to live in harmony, at peace with all men. A lack of harmony can stop people running well. Second, we are to strive after holiness, without which no-one will see the Lord. If you are going to need it then, strive for it now.

Thirdly, here the letter to the Hebrews goes way back into the Old Testament to hold up an example of Esau, a man who could have been in the running but became a straggler. How? He was a man whom the world admires. He was tough, a big, hairy man, a hunter. He was right in line for God's blessing. He was the firstborn, one of twins. His twin was holding him; his little hand was grasping the ankle of Esau. Jacob was grasping from his birth, but Esau came out first. Esau therefore was in the running and could have inherited the blessing. One day Esau saw a plate of soup and he was faced with a choice which every young person has to face and many older people too: the choice between *then* and *now*, between the invisible and the visible, between something that is only a promise and something you can actually have. Between the spiritual and the physical, between the spirit and the flesh, and Esau made the fatal choice.

From that moment he was out of the running. As the firstborn he should have been the father of Israel. He should have been right in line for God's chosen people. Esau should have been the one, but he wasn't. He was disqualified from running. That is why one of the most sober texts in the New Testament is at the end of 1 Corinthians 9. Paul says, "Lest having preached to others I should myself be disqualified from running." That's the literal translation, to be "disqualified from running". No prize for those disqualified.

One of the most humiliating events in my childhood

comes back to me vividly. I have never been able to run far and fast. The Lord blessed me with flat feet. So I have to accept this and live with it. I remember there was one race on school sports day when the entire school had to run four times around the sports field but we were all handicapped according to age, not according to flat feet. I remember us setting off and after two rounds I was all in, and the dear Sergeant Major, who was our PT instructor, got hold of me and pulled me out of that race in front of all the parents, and I have never felt so humiliated. That is what the letter is talking about here. Getting disqualified; pulled out of the race; pulled out of the running —because all of us can be Esaus. What did Esau do? He just exchanged spirit for flesh. He wanted his happiness and satisfaction now.

So the letter says quite practically: Don't be immoral, don't be idolatrous, don't be ungodly like Esau. It is people who have been in the running who now have lost sight of the goal and who are just grabbing satisfaction now. Notice this: such a person in a fellowship becomes a bitter root. I have heard many interpretations of this root of bitterness, and most of them, I think, are wrong. It is often interpreted today as someone who has become critical or resentful. Well, there is plenty of teaching in the Bible about Christians who get critical and resentful, but that is not a root of bitterness. The word "bitterness" doesn't mean emotional bitterness. Bitterness here means "poisonous; a bitter root." If you are collecting wild roots in the Middle East for your dinner, you can so easily pick the wrong one which is bitter to taste and when you put it in the stew it poisons. There is such an account from Elijah's day. They picked a bitter root by mistake and it poisoned the whole stew. What is being said here is that a fellowship that is running the race can be poisoned by one person within it becoming an "Esau" and that root has got to be taken out and uprooted because it is going to hinder all the others and they are going to stop running. When they see that a Christian can simply live for the things of this world and forget about the future, it is a poison—it corrupts, it defiles, it spreads. It contaminates until the whole fellowship can just be running that less fast.

It is a serious word and we need to remember it because I am not just running the race privately. We are all running together; we are all looking to Jesus and therefore we cannot afford a single "Esau". The tragedy is that Esau lived to regret what he had done but could never repent of it. Do you know the difference between regret and repentance? Regret is in your heart; repentance starts in your mind. Literally, the word "repentance" means "change of mind". The tragedy is that someone can regret the consequences of having been disqualified, and shed bitter tears as Esau did, but they cannot change their mind about what they did. One has known this in personal experience, and the tragedy is they cannot rethink their position or see it for what it is, and it has put them out of certain things. It is true to life that if you are disqualified from running you cannot get back into the race.

We have finished this portion of our study on a fairly serious note, haven't we? But life has a finality about it. Don't let us kid ourselves that we can drop out of the race and drop into it at will. The Bible tells us that Esau was disqualified. He chose to get out of the running and then when he regretted it and wanted to get back in he could not do so. So strengthen those feeble knees, make strong the arm, look to Jesus, and let us strip off every handicap that could cling to us, everything that could hold us back — let us run the race with perseverance. He endured everything. Why? Because of the joy set before him. Look what a joy is set before us. We may have to do without certain pleasures here. We may not have as happy a life as some non-Christians. Sometimes we envy them and we say, "Look at my next door neighbour — doesn't seem to bother about godliness or holiness but he enjoys himself. Ah, but it is a slippery slope. Psalm 73 puts the picture right, "Then I went into the sanctuary of God and I perceived their end. Truly, you have set them in a slippery place. But me, you will hold me with your hand and afterward receive me to glory."

I can put up with it now. I have seen the balance; I have seen the race; I have seen the goal; I have seen the prize. I am going to keep my eyes fixed there until I can say one day: I have finished the course, I have kept the faith. Henceforth, there is laid up for me a crown.

10

Mt. SINAI AND Mt. ZION
Read 12:18 – 29

A. THEIR EXPERIENCE – FEELINGS (12:18–21)
1. Mt Zion (on earth)
   a. Visible b. Audible c. Tangible
2. Fear
   a. Israel terrified b. Moses trembling
B. OUR EXALTATION – FAITH (12:22–29)
1. Mt Zion (in heaven)
   a. Angels b. Spirits c. Jesus
2. Fear
   a. Obedience b. Reverence

One of the greatest dangers in the Christian life is of going back to one's old life, reverting to type. There are two ways of doing this, one deliberate and the other unintentional. Hebrews chapter 6 deals with those who, having tasted of the powers of the age to come, having experienced blessing, quite deliberately and wilfully, knowing what they are doing, turn their back on Christ and go right back and away from him. Hebrews 6 says that for such people there is no hope of repentance. You cannot hope to get them back if they have quite deliberately crucified Christ afresh in that way. That is the kind of choice which, as we have seen, once made may be regretted but cannot be undone, and that was why Esau is mentioned as one who made the fatal choice and years later regretted it but could never undo it.

Most backsliding is as the name implies, sliding. It is done unintentionally, not deliberately, but many of us, as Hebrews puts it in nautical terms, drift back into our old way of thinking and our old way of life. We don't intend to, we lose grip of the anchor, we lower the sails, we stop moving in the direction we should move—things just go wrong and we drift back to where we were. This is very dangerous, hence the plea: "Fix your eyes on Jesus. Get rid of anything which handicaps. Run the race and be determined to get there. Keep your eyes fixed on the goal." As this letter really is saying, it is not just important to have begun to be a Christian, it is vital to continue and complete. That is the urgency of the letter to the Hebrews.

Now the particular problem of backsliding was the problem of converted Jews, and that is why it is the letter to *Hebrews*. They are certainly Christians but they had been Jews. The writer's horrible fear is that they will go back to Judaism — that they will revert to their own religion. Notice that you can backslide into things that are good. They are in danger of backsliding not into irreligion, but into religion. They are not in danger of backsliding into immorality, but into morality of the wrong kind. It is a tragic truth underlined by this whole letter that the good is the enemy of the best. Judaism was a good religion, a moral religion, a godly religion, but it was constantly in conflict with Christianity when Christianity came. It was like new wine in old wineskins. God wants the best for you. The best is Christ. You can live a religious and a moral life and still not know the best that God has for you in Jesus Christ.

So the author wrote to these converted Jews and he kept drawing a contrast between Moses and Jesus, between the old religion and the new one. Both of them were good, both of them were from God, but when you have got the best one, the good one becomes a bad one to follow. The key word in the letter to the Hebrews is "better". Christianity is better than all religion, including Judaism, because Christ is better than any other religious leader.

Let me run through the seven contrasts we have had so far in this letter to try and pick up the threads. Contrast number one: Jesus is better than all the prophets. They brought God's Word in bits and pieces, but when Jesus came, God spoke to us as a whole picture.

Secondly, Jesus is far better than the angels; all of them put together, thousands of them. Why? Because at their best the angels are just servants, he is the Son.

Next, Jesus is better than the great pioneers, the apostles of the Old Testament, Moses and Joshua. Why? Because both of them failed in the thing they set out to do. Moses set out to bring the people into the Promised Land and he didn't get them there. Joshua set out to bring them into rest, but he didn't get them there. Jesus brings us into the Promised Land of rest, so he is better.

The next contrast was between Jesus and all the priests of the Old Testament. All the priests of Aaron came and went, and they failed to get people right with God. Jesus came as a priest after the order of Melchizedek and he brought us to God and he remains our priest forever.

The next contrast was between buildings—the old building in the Old Testament and the one which we use today, the heavenly sanctuary. We have better premises and better promises than they had in the Old Testament, so why go back to an earthly sanctuary?

The next contrast was between all the sacrifices of the blood of bulls and goats slain on many altars, year in, year out, and one once for all sacrifice that has covered the sins of the whole world when Jesus died on a cross. How much better!

The next contrast was between all the believers of the Old

Testament and the pioneer and perfecter of our faith, Jesus. However wonderful the example Abraham and Moses and Noah and Joshua and all the others gave, these were great men of faith, but they were not pioneers of faith and they were not perfecters of faith. They were simply examples of faith. But we have a pioneer of faith who starts us off, and we have a perfecter of faith who finishes us off, and so we look to him.

Now for all these seven reasons — better than prophets, angels, apostles, priests, tabernacles, sacrifices, believers — it is much better to be a Christian than a Jew. Why then go back? It is this danger of backsliding we are exploring. Now when he has drawn all these contrasts, the writer has had to steer a very delicate line. There is something now that I feel very strongly and deeply is cursing the life of our churches. It is getting right the relationship between the Old Testament and the New Testament. If you get that wrong, then church life goes badly wrong. They are both from God, they both came from the same God, they are both truth. How do we relate them?

There are two wrong ways of relating them. The first is to have too little contrast between the two and to lump them together indiscriminately, so as to take the same value judgments from Old and New Testaments. For example, Seventh Day Adventists have put their members under the legalism of a weekly Sabbath on Saturday. Why? Because they have got the Old and the New Testaments too close together, and they put Christians under the Old.

Consider the historic attitude of the Dutch Reformed Church to apartheid. If you trace that back, it was due to getting the Old and New Testament confused, and taking some teaching from the Old Testament and applying it in Christian circles.

Let us come even nearer home: why are there churches in

England that have priests, altars and incense, which belonged to the Mosaic Law and are obsolete in Christ? The answer is that we have got the Old and the New Testament too much on the level.

To come right near home, I believe that a weekly Sabbath day is part of the Old Testament and is only a copy of the reality. The reality is to enter into the Sabbath rest in Christ, whereby we cease from our own works and we observe a Sabbath every day of the week and enjoy the Sabbath rest that belongs to the people of God. But how often evangelical Christians have got bogged down in questions of Sunday observance, and they have done it on the grounds of the Old Testament and not the New. It is getting the Old and the New Testament too close together that has led to all these mistakes and many others.

But now look at the other, which concerns me far more deeply, and that is getting the Old and New Testament too far apart — drawing such a contrast between the two that you set them over against each other and reach the point where you say: "The God of the Old Testament and the God of the New are two different Gods." Now that is far more common in church life today. I find it among the ministers and clergy. It is a heresy that is as old as about the second or third century AD. A man called Marcion was the first to start talking like this. His line was: "The God of the Old Testament is a horrible God, he's an ogre, he's a monster, he's a bloodthirsty bully. He orders the slaughter of innocent people, and he's a cruel God, and that's not the God that I meet in the New Testament. I meet a loving, kind Father of our Lord Jesus Christ. Therefore, the Old Testament gives a false picture of God. It's a record of people's false understanding of God, and what we need is the God of Jesus." Have you heard that said?

People like that go on to say, "God would never send

anybody to hell. The God of the Old Testament might, but not the God of the New Testament." This is the kind of tension that is set up. I notice that people who draw this false distinction and draw the contrast too sharply cannot accept all the New Testament either. They don't like the book of Revelation, for a start, because the God of the book of Revelation is too like the God of the Old Testament. Then they don't like quite a bit in Paul because they said, "Paul was a bit too Old Testament, and was a bit old-fashioned in his thinking about God." Then they find there are bits in the Gospels they can't even take either. They reduce it down to some kind of sentimental grandfather created in their own image.

Such people will never preach from the last half of Hebrews 12. They will pick their text but you will never hear this passage expounded, because it rings of the "Old Testament God". Consider the last sentence in it, "For our God is a consuming fire." Now if you didn't know where that came from, you would think it came from the Old Testament. Well it does, it comes three times in the Old Testament—in Leviticus, in Exodus, in Deuteronomy. You might say, "That's an Old Testament conception of God. We Christians don't think of God like that." But this is written to Christians, and this is New Testament, not the Old, and this is an Old Testament quote in the New, and it is the same God through and through. From beginning to end, we have the same God through the whole Bible. Everything said about him in the Old Testament is true and always will be.

Why then do you get a different feel of God in the New Testament than you do in the Old? —because you do, and we have got to face this very honestly. Why is it that in the Old Testament you get an impression of a God you want to run away from, and in the New you get an impression of a God you want to run to? Have you had that impression?

Why this difference? Has God changed? No, I'll tell you why. Something quite profound has changed. It is not God, but our experience of God, which has changed.

This underlines a very important truth, and I want you to go deep. I want to underline this important principle. *Never judge God by your experience of him. Judge him by his revelation of himself.* Now what do I mean by that? I mean that your experience of a person can be grossly misleading if it is limited. We experience one aspect of each other's life when we are officially in church and in meetings. We experience another one when we have got to live together. Your experience of a person may never have included seeing a them lose their temper or get really angry. Somebody may come to you and say, "I saw that person last week and, my, were they angry!" You could say, "Impossible, impossible, I have never known them angry." But that does not prove a thing except that you have never known them angry. It doesn't prove they couldn't be. Do you see what I'm saying? In the Old Testament they experienced a very great deal of the wrath of God. That is how we know that the wrath of God is real. If I have not experienced that, that doesn't mean it doesn't exist. If I have never seen God as fire that doesn't mean he isn't fire. If I have never met God as Judge that does not mean he isn't Judge. It simply means that I haven't had experience of that side of his character. The fact is that Christians have not experienced the side of God's character that the Jews did in the Old Testament, but it is still there and it is still real, and we could experience it. We should thank God that we haven't, but we draw up our picture of God not from our experience of God, but from what he says he is and what he has done.

Let me focus this in even more. I have never experienced the total destruction of my society by flood, but Noah did. Now am I to say that God would never do that because I have not experienced it? Am I to say that God would never destroy an entire society with water simply because I never saw it and I wasn't there? Many preachers do this and they say, "God isn't that kind of a God, I've not experienced that kind of a God. He isn't that kind of a God to me, and therefore I don't believe it." But listen, God said, "While the earth remains, I'll never do that again." "While the earth remains" doesn't mean he isn't the sort of God who would do it. It just means that nobody since Noah's day has experienced that act of God.

Now have I said enough to get you interested and understanding? We are now ready to approach the passage because the whole meaning of this passage is that the experience of the Jews is different from the Christian's experience of God. But what they experienced is still true because God has not changed, and what we experience is still true, and you must put it all together and get the whole picture. Otherwise, the danger is that we do not have enough reverence and awe in our worship. Because we don't experience what the Jews experienced, we tend to be too pally with God. We tend to come to church as if we were going to a cinema because we don't have the same experience of God that they had. That is also the message of Hebrews—God hasn't changed, our experience has changed. So let us develop this. Why is it that we go more by our own experience of God than other people's? The answer is we always trust our own judgment better than other people's. If we have experienced something, we will accept that with far more authority than we accept someone else's experience. So if a man says to me, "Well, to me God is like this" and I say, "Well, that's not how he is to me," who do I take? I am afraid we are so weak humanly that we tend to go by our own experience. Praise God for men of faith who are prepared to go by other people's experience, who are prepared to believe that God is the kind of God whom Noah experienced, whom Abraham experienced, whom Moses experienced, and to take this Bible as a book of their experience and believe that as well, and have a balanced approach to Almighty God.

Let us look first then at their experience and we go back to the most important event in Jewish history—the day that God got married. The ceremony occurred in the middle of a most barren place. It took place in Sinai, in that peninsula where people can die within days of thirst and lack of food. There, among those barren mountains, God got married to Israel and formed a covenant relationship betwixt him and them. They were in a marriage bond, and from then on God called himself "Your Husband", and he called Israel "my wife". When they went after other gods he accused them of adultery.

It is interesting they went after other gods called "Baal" which means "husband," and "Astarte", which means "wife". Through the prophets, God used to thunder to them, "I am your Husband." He had to say to a preacher called Hosea, "Hosea, go out and marry a prostitute," and then when everybody knows about the scandal—can't you see the headlines, "Preacher Marries Prostitute"—"Then," he says, "You tell them that's what all of them are doing. They've become unfaithful to me. They're like a prostitute wife to me."

I want you to try and imagine that place. There is a sort of sandy plane, a valley with a flat, sandy floor and a few stunted trees, about five miles long and about a mile wide. It is surrounded by horrible dry rocks, but at the end of the valley there is an unusual mountain which the Arabs still call Jebel Musa, "the hill of God and Moses". This mountain rises sheer from the sandy floor and it towers about four or five thousand feet up.

God was on that mountain and he said, "Don't come near

this mountain, don't touch it. If even an animal comes and touches it you must kill that animal." That was where the marriage took place. So Moses erected a fence about six feet out from the mountain so people would not be in danger, even animals would be kept off. This was where they met God face to face. This was their experience of God and it was an experience of their senses. Only one sense was not in it, and that was the sense of taste. It was a tangible, physical experience of God to their senses. They saw darkness and a storm, there were black thunderclouds above them. Their sense of touch was involved—it was a mountain that could be touched, and yet must not be touched. Their sense of smell— it was burning. There is evidence of volcanic activity in that area. They heard thunder and then they heard a sound that later they described as the nearest thing to a trumpet blast.

Now how would you feel if you came to church and we saw those things and heard those things, and smelled those things — if you smelled burning right now, if you heard thunder flashes, if the sky was black, and if the building was on the move (because there was a mini earthquake there)? Would you then feel rather differently? Hebrews says you ought to feel like that anyway. You ought to approach God like that when you go to church because he has not changed. The only thing that has changed is that we don't have sense experience of him. Do you see? We have experience of him in another dimension, but he is just the same.

So that was their experience. God's presence was real physically. You could touch, smell, hear and see that God was right there, and everybody knew it. Therefore, secondly, their experience was not only tangible, it was terrifying. As soon as they got there, they didn't want to be there—they wanted to run, they wanted to go home, they wanted to get up and go. They begged Moses, "Tell God not to go on speaking. Tell him not to talk to us, we can't stand it." They were terrified out of their wits, and so would you be if God showed himself physically like this. Their reaction was not to come near to him, but to pull away. Their reaction was due to this horrible fear.

Supposing you knew that anybody who happened to touch a particular wall would be stoned to death immediately, wouldn't you keep to the back of the auditorium? Of course you would. The whole situation produced fear, terror, and they wanted to pull away from God. Even Moses himself, we are told, trembled with fear. Now what the letter to the Hebrews is saying is this: Do you ever tremble before God? Do you ever do so?

I have sat behind someone in a meeting and watched him come under the power of the Holy Spirit, and I watched him come under conviction. He was a grown man in his forties and he was shaking, trembling in his seat. Thank God when we realise that God is exactly the same as he was in Sinai and that we don't have to see, and touch, and smell to know that God is that real. So it was a tangible experience and a terrifying experience. You may have come to church for years and never have had such an experience. That does not mean God has changed, it means your experience is different, that's all.

Now let us look at our experience, which is so very, very different. Our experience is intangible, not tangible. It is of things not seen, not heard, not touched, not smelled, not tasted—not physically. All our experience is based on faith, which goes beyond the senses. It is not therefore, sensory experience. Our experience is different. We have come to a mountain, but not a physical mountain, we have come to another one. We have not come to an earthly mountain; we have come to a heavenly mountain. I cannot see it but I have come to it. Interestingly enough, we have not come to a heavenly counterpart of Mount Sinai, but a heavenly counterpart of Mount Zion. Do you understand the difference there? Mount Sinai is the place where God gives his demands, his laws. Mount Zion is the place where you are at home with God. It is a heavenly mountain, not an earthly one.

That is our experience— and it is totally different from their experience. But God is the same. We have not only come to a mountain, we have come to a city. It is crowded with population. We meet God in a city, not in a wilderness — a mountain on which there are buildings, not an earthly city but a heavenly one again.

Like Abraham, we look for a city whose builder and maker is God. But we have come there; we are already there. From that point of view we are not marching to Zion, we are sitting there. You have come to these. Not "you will come" but, "you have come". So we come to a mountain, we come to a city, and by faith we see these. Now far from putting us off, what we have already experienced has just drawn us closer. For we have come to the living God as they did —same living God. They came and they wanted to pull away, and they didn't want to listen. We come and we want to draw near and we want to listen. Why? Well, I'll tell you why. We don't see God sitting alone on a mountain. We see him surrounded with people—a city full of people. And we see thousands upon thousands of angels. You have come to these. You have come to the living God, and you have come to myriads of angels in a joyous assembly celebrating. That is what makes us want to celebrate. How different our experience. When the Jews came to the living God by himself at Mount Sinai they didn't want to celebrate, but we do. Interesting, you know, that deep down the human heart wants to celebrate, wants to be joyful.

So when the Jews had that experience of God at Sinai they didn't find it joyful. So what did they do? As soon as Moses got up there, they built a golden calf and they said, "Now let's have singing and dancing," and they had it around the golden calf. But we don't get tempted to put up a golden calf, we enjoy God, we celebrate now.

These angels started singing when you were born again. They were celebrating up there as soon as you repented of your sins. We have come to all these thousands upon thousands of angels, and they are celebrating — that doesn't make me want to pull back, it makes me want to join them and join in the fun.

We have also come to the church of the firstborn. Now that little expression "firstborn" — what does it mean? In any family in Bible days one person in the family inherited, and it was the firstborn. A father's business was inherited by the firstborn—we have come to the church of the firstborn and every member of the church of Christ is the firstborn because everyone is going to inherit, and everyone is going to have it all. To come to the church of the firstborn does not put me off, it just draws me closer. The privilege of being part of Christ's church, and finding everywhere in the world I have come to this church of the firstborn! I have come to be with people.

Then, secondly, I find I come to the spirits of just men made perfect. What does that mean? That refers to men and women who have died and who are now perfect. They were righteous on earth, now they have been made perfect. They are not embodied yet, because they are waiting for their resurrection body; we will all get that body at the same time. That is heaven, isn't it? It is hell to be with imperfect people forever, but it is heaven to be with perfect people forever. You have come to the spirits of just men made perfect.

So, to summarise: when you are in church you are in the church of the firstborn. There are thousands upon thousands of angels rejoicing and watching what happens in the service.

They rejoice if one person comes to Christ. We have come to spirits of just men made perfect. We are surrounded with a great cloud of witnesses, the communion of saints. That doesn't put me off. The living God in the midst of his angels, his church, his saints—what more could you ask? That is my experience of God. It is totally different from the Jewish experience of Mount Sinai. Why? Has God changed? Not in the slightest.

You have come to the living God, the Judge of all men, it says here — the same God that they met at Sinai, the Judge of all men—exactly the same title, exactly the same God. They came and they met the Judge and they wanted to run away. I come and I meet the Judge and I want to run to him. Why? Not just the crowd of angels and people around him, but there is something else. I have come to Jesus, the Mediator of a new covenant. His blood shouts louder than Abel's did, that is why. I am not filled with terror. Why not? Because the blood of Jesus speaks louder.

Do you know all the blood shed in the Old Testament cries for vengeance, punishment, retribution? All the blood that was shed, even the sacrifices of burnt offerings—because they did not take away sins they simply spoke more loudly about the vengeance that would come, about the price that needs to be paid, about the cost of sin which has to be paid in blood. Every bit of blood in the Old Testament cried for vengeance, punishment.

But when Jesus died, his blood cried for mercy. Even the first bloodshed in the Bible, the blood of Abel—killed, murdered by his own brother. In the first family there was a murder. God said to Cain, "Your brother's blood cries to me from the ground." What did it cry for? Punishment of Cain.

Do you know this hymn: "Abel's blood for vengeance pleaded to the skies, but the blood of Jesus for my pardon cries"? In other words, that which stands between me and this God of Sinai is the blood of Jesus. Even at Sinai they took the blood of animals. They sprinkled the fence, they sprinkled the mountain, they sprinkled the people—there was blood everywhere but all it did was remind them of punishment. But not now. I have come to Mount Zion and now the blood is sprinkled on me, not for vengeance, not for punishment, but for pardon and mercy. The blood of Jesus stands between me and the living God. I am protected.

Therefore, here am I, in the same position as a Jew at Sinai, a sinner, facing the living God. I am not running away and I am not terrified, because I have come to the Mediator of a new covenant. There is someone between me and God, and there is something between me and God. The someone is the Mediator, Jesus, and the something is his sprinkled blood. So I am not frightened to worship the living God. I have come to Mount Zion, not Mount Sinai, and my experience is different.

Now I come to the last point I want to make here, and it is the serious point of the whole study. *We are in a greater danger, therefore, than the Jews of Sinai. Why? Because the thought of God's holiness was so obvious to them that the fear of God was in them. It is not so obvious to us, and therefore we, with the greater privilege of a more wonderful experience of God, can take him less seriously.*

If you went to church and there was fire and thunder and trumpet blasts and the building shook, maybe you would take more notice of God than you are taking right now. That is the danger, and it is an awful danger. The danger is that because God doesn't manifest himself in the same way, we take his Word lightly; we don't pay so much attention to it.

The letter to the Hebrews says quite simply: If they did not escape when they refused him who warned them on earth, how much less will we if we turn away from him who warns us from heaven.

They had an earthly, tangible warning. We have a spiritual, heavenly warning. That places a greater responsibility, not lesser, on our response to God's Word. There should be a greater sense of reverence in us, not less. There should be a deeper sense of listening and obeying his word than there was in that dramatic surrounding of thunder and lightning, fire, and the rest.

Yet here is the tragedy: looking at any congregation in England, do you get the sense that they have come to that kind of a God? That they are hanging on every word because their very life depends on it — that it is a matter of life and death; that to play around with the word of God is to go and touch the holy mountain?

Our experience is different, but the revelation is the same. His word is the same and his word states that at Mount Sinai he shook the earth. But his word states he is going to shake not only the earth but space and all the planets in it — the heavens are going to be shaken. God is going to take this whole universe and shake it. Not just the world, your church building will shake; England will shake. There will not only be an earthquake, but isn't it interesting, we have no word in our vocabulary for "heaven quake" yet that is what is going to happen.

I think I would like to just have the feel of what an earthquake is like, and yet on the other hand I wouldn't. Because one lady told me she had been in a severe one and she said, "I was terrified — the house in which I was living was shaking, so I ran into the garden and the house collapsed behind me like a pack of cards. I was running down the road and the road was shaking and cracking before me. I saw a car driving along and the earth opened, and the car went down the chasm and the earth closed. Now if an earthquake can produce that, it is nothing compared with what God says he is going to do. The same God who shook Sinai will shake the stars, he is going to shake the whole universe. Why? To shake everything out of it that is not lasting, that the things can remain which are unshaken. Now what will you lose when he shakes the universe? You will lose your house. You will lose your car. You will lose your business. We will lose the church buildings. All created things will be lost. What will you keep when he shakes the whole universe and only the unshaken things remain? Listen, we who are receiving a kingdom that cannot be shaken should be thankful. In that day every government will be shaken out of this universe. Every national state will be shaken away. There is only one kingdom which will remain, and it is the kingdom of heaven, the kingdom to which we belong. Mount Zion will stand. The heavenly city, Jerusalem, will stand when all other cities are shaken away—that is the truth. I have not experienced this and therefore my temptation is to think that my church building is strong enough to survive forever. My house is so stable that I tend to think it is going to stand there forever. This earth seems so solid I think it is going to be here forever. I take it more lightly, and I don't take it seriously and I dismiss it and say, "Oh, well, I won't be around when it happens," and that is the danger. But if I had come to Mount Sinai, I wouldn't feel that way. I would feel that the whole thing could shake at any minute, that it could go any minute, and that I could go with it unless I am right with God.

Therefore, it is important to know that God destroyed the earth with water — he has promised to destroy it once more, and the heavens too, with fire. People laughed at that for centuries until a scientist said, some years ago, that if we could get the right apparatus and trigger the mechanism, this universe could be subject to a chain reaction of nuclear destruction, which would dissolve it in fire in less than forty minutes. We are forty minutes away from total destruction.

Not just the earth, but the entire universe. That is how you feel when you meet the living God. For you see, God is not only Father, he is fire too. The tragedy is that those whose experience has not included fire latch onto the Father and forget the fire. He is Father, yes, he is the Father of our Lord Jesus, and he is my Father too, and your Father too. But he is fire — my earthly father was never fire, but God is consuming fire.

I watched a few minutes of a television programme depicting a very exciting moment. A geographical society explorer was the first man to climb inside the cone of a live volcano. He donned an asbestos suit. He took a stainless steel wire ladder and they hung it down over the side. Below him there was a seething cauldron of molten lava, and from it there were popping up bits of red-hot rock, ash, and there was poisonous gas. He put on a gas mask, an oxygen mask, then he climbed down into the volcano—the first time a man had done this. He went down and down, and you held your breath as he descended. You knew that at any minute the thing could go up. If it did, that would be the end of him, he would be a little piece of charred cinder.

So, breathless, we watched him go down as he climbed into the very heart of it. In fact he was overcome by the gas and had to be hauled out. Brave, bold man to do such a thing, but what I am saying is this: every time you come to worship, every time you come to the living God, you are climbing down inside a volcano. There is only one thing between you and the fire —you are covered not with an asbestos suit but with the sprinkled blood of Jesus. The ladder you are climbing is faith, and it won't let you down. You can live in the volcano, and you can call the volcano Father—that is amazing.

How do we work this out in practice then? Not by setting the Old Testament against the New and saying, "The God of the fire —that is Mount Sinai, that is the Jews. Not for me. I've got a nice God, a pally God. I can just come to him and chat with him." No, not by doing that, but by recognising that God is still a consuming fire, that he is still going to shake the earth and the heavens once more, and shake out of it everything and everyone who is not eternal —by recognising that and then coming to God with two things in your heart, two attitudes of heart and mind. Hebrews is teaching us to come to him with these two things. Firstly, reverence and awe. In coming to church you stepped into a volcano, you came near the living God. It is of his mercies that we are not consumed. He would just need to say one word, and the entire building and everyone in it could go up in smoke. That is the God you come to. So learn the meaning of the word "awe". (Hence the meaning of the word "awful" and, "O, how awful is this place"; how dreadful is this place. Secondly, approach him with gratitude — that you can live in this volcano, that you have perfect protection from the fire; that you will not be burned up when everything else is; that you are covered with the blood of Jesus, and that you can climb right into the presence of God by faith, and you can stand there. Let us be thankful and approach with reverence and awe.

11

GOING ON DOING AND BEING
Read 13:1 – 7

A. THE LOVE THAT GOES ON DOING (13:1–7)
1. Loving believers (1)
    a. Each other   b. As brothers
2. Entertaining strangers (2)
    a. Humans   b. Angels
3. Suffering empathy (3)
    a. Prisoners   b. Persecuted
4. Honouring marriage (4)
    a. No adultery   b. No fornication
5. Avoiding covetousness (5–6)
    a. What he says   b. What we say
6. Remembering leaders (7)
    a. Their life   b. Their faith
B. THE LORD WHO GOES ON BEING (13:8)
1. Yesterday
2. Today
3. For ever

It is a very popular idea that it doesn't matter what you believe as long as you are sincere. The story that brings home to me more than anything else the falsity of that statement, is the story of two little babies born in a maternity hospital somewhere in the southeast of England. They both needed an urgent operation. They were rushed to the operating theatre, and there the babies were prepared. The nurse on duty was asked to go and fill a syringe with a certain drug to give to them to prepare them.

She went to the cupboard and she filled it from the wrong bottle. They brought the drug, they injected the two babies, and they died a few minutes later. At the inquiry, the nurse said these words—and I quote her exactly: "I sincerely believed I had the right bottle." But if you are sincerely wrong then your beliefs can do damage to yourself and to other people. For you see, the real truth is that it is not a man's behaviour that makes a man, but what he believes.

Belief is the inside of him; behaviour is the outside. If you change a man's outside, and change his behaviour, you have not changed him. You may have done nothing to touch the real person. Therefore the Bible, with true insight into human nature, teaches that if you can change a man's beliefs, then his behaviour can be put right in the proper way. Indeed, this is fundamental to life. All commercial advertising is based on the fact that if you change a person's beliefs you will change their behaviour. Take the government's anti-smoking campaign—the shock films that are put out on television are designed to change your beliefs. You see, one of the most fundamental beliefs of human nature in its fallen state is this: it could never happen to me. No matter how many disasters we see in other people, or what tragedies we read about, there is something in us that says "It will never happen to us." But the anti-smoking propaganda is to change that belief until you believe it could happen to you. Once you have changed your belief, you are likely to change your habit.

So the whole of life is concerned really with our belief, and only then are we in a position to change our behaviour. This is the pattern in the Bible again and again. In epistle after epistle there is a whole section on belief first, and then and only then are questions of behaviour tackled. That is the only way in which you can finally redeem human nature. Change the inside and then you can change the outside. Paul's letter to the Ephesians is a particularly clear example of this. Chapters 1–3 are all about our belief and our salvation. Chapters 4–6 are all about working it out in our relationships, into our leisure, into our social life, and so on.

Now the letter to the Hebrews is exactly the same. Up to the end of chapter 12 we have been dealing with your beliefs—what you believe about Jesus as far better than angels, priests, prophets, offering a better sacrifice than of animals, worshipping in a better sanctuary than an earthly building — all *better*. Now have you believed that? If so, then you have joined a long line of heroes of faith: Noah, Abraham, Moses, Gideon, Samson, Barak and all the rest of them—you have joined a line of those whose belief changed, and therefore whose behaviour also changed.

The final definition of faith is given in chapter 12, at the beginning. Faith is stripping off everything that handicaps you and the sin which clings to you, and looks to Jesus and runs the race to finish it. All through this letter we have had the emphasis on finishing what you have started, on continuing the faith, on completing the course. It is one thing to begin to be a Christian, it is quite another to go on after five years, ten years, twenty years, thirty years, and to keep on going on. Somebody in my congregation told me they had been walking with the Lord for seventy years—that is a good race to run, and this is the whole emphasis.

Now, in chapter 13, down to earth with a bump. The tragedy is that some people think we have reached a kind of postscript that you put at the end of a letter. But that is not the case. It is fundamental to the whole thing. It is not a practical postscript; it is working out what God has worked in. "Work out your own salvation, for it is God who works in you" — that is the balance of scripture. Therefore, having discussed beliefs and got our faith centred on Christ, the writer of this letter is saying: now work it out. He is so practical. Work it out in the use of your home. Work it out in your marriage bed. Work it out with your bank account.There are so many things that he says here which are so utterly down to earth that I make no apology for being very earthy. We have been heavenly—looking to Jesus, gazing at heavenly sanctuaries; looking at angels; seeing things that others cannot see. Now earth, where it has all got to be worked out—because, frankly, if our religion doesn't work out on Monday then it is no good on Sunday. If it doesn't work out in our house and in our marriage and in our finance, then it doesn't work out in church either. It has got to be a practical faith. "If he is not Lord of all, he's not Lord at all." That is a neat little cliché that I think sums up everything I want to say here.

Let us look at this chapter in a rather novel way. I have pointed out that it is working it out practically. There are many exhortations here to us to do certain things in our daily life. But I am going to make them negative instead of positive. They are all positive exhortations, to do this or do that. But if I make them negative and put it in the negative form there is a list of things in this chapter that will tell you when you are backsliding. There are twelve signs in this chapter of a person who is no longer looking to Jesus, who has lost hold of the anchor within the veil, and is drifting towards the rocks.

There are rocks described in this chapter on which a life could founder. Any one of them could happen in any Christian's life as soon as we stop looking at Jesus, like Peter walking on the Sea of Galilee. When he looked at Jesus he could walk on top of the sea, but when he took his eyes off Jesus, the sea got on top of him. This is the profound thing in life: as soon as we look at Jesus we get on top of life and nothing can get on top of us. But take your eyes off Jesus and things get on top of us very quickly.

Here are six of the things that could be a sign to you that you are drifting towards the rocks, that you have taken your eyes off Jesus. *First, if you lose your love for your fellow Christians you must have taken your eyes off Jesus.* For the first positive exhortation here is to keep on loving each other as brothers. Now that is something you cannot do if you are not looking to Jesus, not continuing in the faith, not looking to him and not trusting him to help.

Let us go back to the day you became a Christian. What happened? You began to love Jesus, but one other thing happened as well, which surprised you: you started to love his people. You felt that you belonged to them, you had affection for them; you wanted to be with them. To love Christ is to love his people, just as to hate Christ is to hate his people. The two are so bound together—you can't love the Lord without loving his people. You are a liar if you say you love the Lord and you don't love your brother. You see, you can't love Christ without loving all those you see in Christ. If you are looking to Christ you will see everybody who is in him, and you will love what you see. So in your early days as a Christian, you began to love every other Christian, whatever age, whatever temperament—we just belonged. If we take our eyes off Jesus that does not last. The tragedy is that you then revert to the most that human love can do, and that is to love those you like. When you joined God's family, you didn't choose your brothers and sisters, and they are a funny lot.

A dear lady, after every church meeting would say, "Good night Pastor." Then she would shake her head with a rueful smile, and in sheer love she would say, "You know, Pastor, the Lord has a funny family, hasn't he?" I had to agree after some church meetings, and maybe people thought that about me too. Therefore, if you are not looking to Jesus you stop loving all your fellow Christians and you only love those you like. It is not long before that develops into cliques, and groups, snobbery and all kinds of things. It can get right inside a church.

So the very first sign that you are slipping from Christ and that your faith is slipping and that you are not looking to him is that you can no longer love all your fellow Christians. You begin to be put off some. You haven't the capacity because at a human level you can only like certain people. Nobody can go beyond that, so at the human level you choose your set and you stay within the set. In a large church you can do that even more than in a small church if you are not careful because you can just stay with your own group. I want you to ask yourself: are you always talking to the same people after the service? Some do, I have noticed, and some mix with anybody.

Ask yourself this question: am I loving every fellow Christian? Am I going on loving those brothers? After all, we are going to live together in heaven. We belong to each other as a family. The kind of love that we are to have for each other is neither heterosexual nor homosexual, it is to be brotherly love for which the Greeks had two words *phileo* (love) and *adelphos* (brother) joined in the Greek word *philadelphia* which is used here. When they founded Philadelphia in America they hoped it was going to be a city of brotherly love. That is a city where you don't walk the streets at night now. There is no city on earth that can be called "philadelphia", but there is a new city coming that could — new Jerusalem, where everybody will live in love as brothers.

As long as we are looking to Christ, we have the privilege of anticipating that and enjoying it here, and being brothers now. Do you see what happens? If you look towards Christ, you are looking towards the face of every other person who is looking to Christ. But as soon as you take your eyes off

Christ you cannot see some of his people. But turn away from Christ and there are going to be some in the circle you will not see as brothers. That is the first sign of backsliding. If you are finding that once you could get on with Christians better than you can get on with them now, ask yourself, "When did I take my eyes off Jesus?" It is the first sign.

The second sign is that you will begin to limit your hospitality if you take your eyes off Jesus.

What you do with your house, your home, is a direct reflection of your relationship to the Lord Jesus Christ. What are you doing with your home? Once again it doesn't say that you will cease hospitality if you take your eyes off Jesus. But what you will do is this: you will limit your hospitality to a known circle of people you already relate to. You will not entertain strangers to any great degree. If you are looking at Christ you find that you have got a love for the stranger and you want him within your gates. So your home becomes a place where if anybody lived with you they would constantly meet new people, not the old round, the same set.

Jesus gave us a solemn warning: don't invite to your homes people who will just feel under obligation to invite you back, so that it becomes a kind of mutual meal club. Don't do that. Invite those to your home who won't invite you back and who can't invite you back — but stretch out your hospitality. Don't just limit it to your set; welcome the stranger. After all, Jesus said, "I was a stranger and you took me in." So a sign of backsliding is that our homes begin to be limited to a particular set of people. No longer are they open to strangers, people passing through, but only to those who will invite us back, to those who belong to our group.

The great privilege of entertaining strangers is mentioned here. It is a privilege. You never quite know what blessing will come into your home if you open it to a stranger. Some have told me again and again what a privilege it has been to invite a total stranger who has attended the church service and to have said to them, "Come back home for lunch." I have been told: "You know, I had no idea what a blessing it would be to us. I had no idea what they would bring into our home." Of course you hadn't, because you hadn't had them before. You could even, says the scripture, have a supernatural visitor from heaven, because an angel can appear on earth exactly as a human being appears. You could have had in your home an angel from heaven. When you get to heaven you would see them again, you would recognise them and say, "Why, you came to our house to lunch." That happened to Abraham, it happened to Gideon and it is quite clear that it is anticipated that it will happen in the New Testament days as well. So entertain strangers, for some have had angels in their home. You can't have an angel in your house without receiving a blessing.

The third sign of backsliding is that you forget Christians who suffer for their faith, a group that we need to remember constantly.

If you take your eyes off Jesus, you will take your eyes off those who suffer in his name. They need prayer, they need support, and they need concern. In fact, the letter to the Hebrews says, "Remember those in prison as if you were in prison, and remember those who are ill treated as if you were being ill treated." Do you know the meaning of the word "sympathy"? It is to suffer with someone as if you were in their shoes.

People in prison will be forgotten unless Christians remember them. There are many people who are incarcerated in prisons and labour camps because of Christ. If I take my eyes off Jesus, I will take my eyes off them, because when I look to Jesus I find he is not so much looking at me, he is looking at them. He has a special concern for those who suffer in his name. "Saul, Saul, why persecutest thou me?"

Paul could have said, "Well, I'm not persecuting you, Lord. I am just after these Christians." "But inasmuch as you do it to the least of these, my brethren, you do it to me."

Do you know that the Christian care of those in prison in the early days of the church was so deep that the emperor finally passed the law that anybody visiting someone in prison would be put into prison themselves for the same sentence as the person they visited? Because, in fact, when the Christians were thrown into jail other Christians brought them food, and in jails in those days they weren't fed. In spite of that, the Christians went on visiting. More and more got thrown into jail.

Are you thinking of Christians under an atheistic regime that is anti-Christian? If you take your eyes off Christ you will forget these people. In fact, you will become so bound up with your own problems, your own suffering, you will just forget others. But the way to cure your own troubles is to think of those with much bigger ones and to remember those in prison and those ill-treated. When did you last pray for Christians in prison?

The fourth sign that a person has taken their eyes of Christ is that they will have a lower view of marriage, and things are likely to go wrong in the marriage.

You see, the simple fact is that God's standards in relationship to marriage and divorce are the strictest there have ever been. Our Lord had the very highest standards in relation to these things. One can state the biblical standards in relation to sex very clearly. There are just two principles and everything flows from them—absolute chastity outside marriage and absolute fidelity inside marriage —that is God's will and pattern.

I tell you, there is no-one who can live up to those standards by human nature alone. Therefore, you will only keep them if you look to Jesus, and therefore if you take your eyes off Jesus they are bound to slip. The world says, "These standards are too high, we must lower the standards to meet the people." But Jesus teaches that we must lift the people to meet the standards. That is his way. It is the way of grace, not the way of ingratiation, and so he has these high standards.

The letter to the Hebrews says, "Let marriage be honoured by all." Now that could mean one of three things. It could mean as over against the view that celibacy is a higher way, a more honourable way, we should remember that marriage is honourable, that it is a valid relationship in God's sight and that Jesus himself honoured it. Though he was never married, the first miracle was turning water into wine at a wedding reception and in this way he honoured the relationship.

Therefore, we should never denigrate marriage. One of Paul's remarks taken right out of context is that it is better to marry than to burn. It can be made to look as if Paul was saying marriage is a sort of second best if you can't avoid it. That is a libel on Paul. If you read it in context he said nothing of the kind. But there is the view that somehow marriage is a little lower than celibacy. It applies very much within Roman Catholic circles, but not there alone. If anything today in our society, we have gone the other way and we regard being single as second best. It is not, it is also a calling. In the Bible being single is a gift of the Spirit and being married is a gift of the Spirit.

A second meaning could be: let it be honoured by loyalty. There was a time you could assume that divorce did not take place in Christian circles, nor remarriage. That picture is changing alarmingly rapidly. For discussion of this, see my book *Remarriage is Adultery Unless....* However unpopular and however out of step with our contemporary society, we are looking to Jesus and therefore marriage is to be honoured.

A third possible meaning to this phrase and it certainly

comes to the next phrase in the letter if it is not in this one, is that marriage is not to be regarded as legalised lust and that marriage is not permission to include every unnatural vice within the marriage bed. It is still holy matrimony. It isn't saying as long as you do anything with your married partner, it's okay. It is saying let marriage still be an honourable thing within the marriage bed.

Any of those three things can happen when you take your eyes off Jesus. All of them mean a lower view of marriage, a lighter view of the vows and loyalty involved in a Christian marriage. It is a sign of taking your eyes off Christ that these things go wrong.

The fifth of the sixth things I want to mention: when you take your eyes off Christ then things go wrong between you and your bank balance, between you and your money.

Somehow the attitude changes from contentment to covetousness. Because by nature we are not content with what we have, by grace we can be. Do you know the greatest profit you could make on a business deal? I'll tell you: godliness with contentment is great gain. Or in simple English: the biggest profit you can make on any deal is to be content with what you have — because this world is full of people who are not content with what they have. The funny thing is that once you turn away from Christ you get bitten by this bug which is there. The great apostle Paul said that he kept all the commandments except one. The one he couldn't keep was, "Thou shall not covet", and that is an intriguing admission.

The Pharisees were said to be lovers of money. Money is not a bad thing. Money is a good thing. It is a very convenient thing. It is much more convenient than barter. It is a very handy thing. It means I can send help very quickly to needy people in other countries. It can do so much good. Money is not the root of all evil — the Bible says that the *love of money* is the root of all evil. To be possessed by your possessions is a very sad form of slavery.

Godliness with contentment—do you think it is easier to be content with a little or content with a lot? I think it is harder to be content with a lot because money has this effect: the more you have, the more you want. It is like a drug. Businessmen I have met who have made enough to last them a lifetime and see them right through retirement and make every provision for their children cannot stop making money. It has bitten them and it becomes a consuming idol. They have just got to go on making money, though they have got ample. It is a disease and I know it can be rationalised—if a business isn't going forward it's going backward, and all the rest. But deep down one has got be very sure that it is not the love of money behind it, the feeling of power at having made a big deal.

So *contentment*—that doesn't mean poverty. The Lord does not say you have got to be poor to be content. But the Bible does say that if you are rich it will be harder, sometimes as hard as for a camel to get through the eye of a needle. It is harder the more you have to be content, but listen to the apostle Paul in Philippians 4, "I have learned in whatever state I am, therein to be content.... I have learned to abound and to be abased...." What an achievement it is to be content! I will tell you how to get it — by looking to the Lord and by saying: They may take everything else away from me, but the one thing they cannot take is the presence of my Lord; the Lord is my helper, and I shall not be afraid — he has said, "I will never leave you nor forsake you", he has promised to care for me, and he has promised to provide everything I need. All these things will be added to me if I seek first his kingdom. Therefore, if I am looking to him I need not fear what man can do to my bank balance.

Which would you rather have: the security of a very large

sum of money but to be without the Lord, or to have him and no money? Who is more secure? So, therefore, a fifth sign of our backsliding is that we develop a wrong attitude to money.

Sixth: if you take your eyes off Christ, you will tend to forget the saints who influenced you in your early Christian life.

How you need to remember them. Memory is a great gift of God. Thank God for it as long as you have it. It may begin to fail, but one of the delightful compensations that God has given us is that you can remember earlier things far better than later things. You can go right back to those early years and remember those great saints who spoke the Word of God to you. Their lives may be an example and an inspiration to you, as well as their lips. Their lips told you the Word of God. That was why they were a good influence on your character. They didn't give you their opinions, they didn't tell you what they thought—they gave you the Word of God. Remember at this moment someone who did that for you. Was it your mother who first taught you to pray and told you about Jesus? Was it a grandparent? Was it a Sunday school teacher? Was it a preacher, a pastor, a Christian friend? When you take your eyes off Christ you will forget that person. Look to Christ and you will remember those who pointed you to him.

It says, "Consider the end of their faith" also translated: "Consider the outcome of their faith." That is one possible meaning of the word "end" but the other possible meaning, which I think is the right one, is this, "Consider the end of their lives of faith. Consider how they died." Because Christianity is not only a way of life, it is a way of death. It is not only to teach us how to live; it is to teach us how to die. Christians die in a different way from others. That is why a man I heard about, when he was nearing the end of his life, called for all his relatives to come and stay with him, saying, "Come and see how a Christian dies." My own father, when he was very seriously ill, was confused and rambling a bit and saying all kinds of things, but one thing he said that was sensible was: "David, please pray that I may die in a Christian way."

Consider the end of their faith, consider how they go out. Not how they started, not how they came in. Some of us have great memories of the end of faith in those who taught us the Word of God. What an example and what an inspiration. When people die looking forward—calm, peaceful, looking forward to being with Jesus, it is so different, as different as a Christian funeral is from other funerals. Any actor will tell you the exit is as important as the entrance. They have their exits and they cease to be an influence, but we are to remember those who have been faithful witnesses to Jesus Christ.

We come to Jesus. Of no other human being can this be said—they are the same yesterday, today, and forever. It is sometimes said as a compliment of a friend: "What I like about them is that they're always the same." You know, you never catch them out. They are always as glad to see you and to help you. They are always ready to listen and so on. But they are not always the same. I know they may not change as much as others do, but they change, and they grow older and life's experiences change their character. Above all, they change in that they change location. There will be a time when you can no longer go to them for help and understanding, and they will be out of your life. There is only one of whom you can say: "He is always the same." Look to him, Jesus Christ, the same yesterday, today and forever.

12

FINAL WORDS
Read 13:8 – 25

A. SOUND DOCTRINE (8–10)
1. Outward food
2. Inward favour
B. SOCIAL DISGRACE (11–14)
1. Outside the city
2. Outside the camp
C. SACRIFICIAL DUTIES (15–16)
1. Praise
2. Provision
D. SUITABLE DEFERENCE (17)
1. Persuaded by
2. Yield to
E. SUPPORTED DELEGATES (18–19)
1. Their responsibility
2. Their return
F. SPIRITUAL DEDICATION (20–21)
1. Your work for him
2. His work in you
G. SENSIBLE DETAILS (22–23)
1. Corresponding
2. Coming
H. STRENGTHENED DISCIPLES (24–25)
1. Greetings for all
2. Grace with all

Hebrews 12 tells us that the race is on for Christians, and it immediately goes on to tell us that the Lord will chastise those whom he loves, that he wants us to run the race, and that he wants us to win for his glory. On a sports field you cannot run a race unless you have the lines marked out. Hebrews 13 is not a postscript with additional pieces of advice that the author has just thought of, it is a thoroughly integrated part of the letter. Hebrews is saying, "Run your race looking to Jesus," then marks out the course for us.

Guidelines are being drawn because just to exhort people to run the race looking unto Jesus doesn't spell it out. How do we run this race? In Hebrews 13 the author is saying these are the lines within which you are to run. We have already seen in this chapter of the epistle six guidelines teaching us how we are to run the race. We are now going to look at the other six.

Here is the first thing: *take your eyes off Jesus and you get carried away by all kinds of strange teaching*. The devil knows that he can attack us in this way and get us stuck on strange and heretical nonsense. It is a tragedy when you meet an orthodox, sound Christian who was running well and when you talk to him you find he has got stuck on something weird; he has become a crank over something. Suddenly one thing has blown up to be the whole of Christian counsel and that one thing has got off balance. It saddens your heart and you think, "How did he get caught by this kind of teaching? Where did he get it from? What books has he been reading? Who has led him astray?"

Test all teaching by looking to Jesus, and see if it fits in with him. Don't get carried away by all kinds of strange teaching. It is often very interesting, even compelling, but believe me, as you run your race you will meet Christians with weird ideas. Don't get carried away. "Don't get blown off course with every puff of doctrine," Paul says. If you are easily carried away by strange ideas, if you have the kind of curious mind that loves to be different, and loves to be just a little unsound, then frankly, a puff of strange doctrine and you are blown off course.

The particular heresy mentioned here is a weird one, which has not troubled us much, so it is a little hard for us to understand. Commentators are puzzled by vv. 9–10. We can say some things—it is obvious that they had become cranks over food, getting weird ideas about diet. Now of course, dietary ideas have often got mixed up with religion. It is true that pagan religion was often tied up with particular foods—meat offered to idols and so on. You know that Jews do not touch pork. There were other unclean and clean foods and they had ceremonial foods — the Passover meal had ceremonial foods and so on. It is quite clear, reading between the lines, that these Christian Hebrews had somehow got all mixed up with dietary laws.

I met such a Christian not long ago and he had become a fanatic about certain vitamin pills. He had blue pills for the morning, pink pills at night, and other coloured pills for something else. It had become bound up with his Christianity, so that he was talking in the same breath about these vitamins and his Christian faith. It is possible to do this—some people believe that Christians should be vegetarians, and there are other things that get tied up with it.

Whatever it was here, Hebrews deals with it in a Jewish way with a Jewish argument to show that Christianity is not primarily concerned with what we eat and drink. The argument is: Look back to your own Jewish background. On the Day of Atonement, which is the heart of your religion, the heart of your ritual, the great annual day of taking away sins, what happened? A sacrifice was offered, the blood was taken into the holy place to make that holy place holy, and then the body of the victim was not eaten. Rather, the body was taken right outside the camp and burned to show that on that day the purification for sin was through blood, not through flesh, and that there was no eating part of it involved at all.

Now that was a Jewish kind of an argument but it was true to their religion. It is saying that Christ fulfils the Day of Atonement. He makes us holy through his blood. His body was taken outside the city wall as the Day of Atonement sacrifice was taken outside the camp. Therefore, Christianity is not a matter of diet. Some of the other offerings of Jews, it is true, they offered to God and they ate part of it themselves, but not this one on the Day of Atonement. It is not a question now of eating. It is an involved argument. It may not just click with us, but what it says is what Paul says in another place: "The Kingdom of God is not food and drink, it is righteousness, and peace, and joy in the Holy Spirit."

Weird teaching can get mixed up with Christianity. Don't listen to Christians who tell you you have got to have a special diet. That is not part of Christian teaching. It is a strange teaching that carries some people away. God has given us all things freely to enjoy, and once Christians start making rules for each other about what they can or can't eat or drink, they are getting away from Christ.

From all this this argument we can learn two things about strange teachings. They are characteristic of all weird ideas that distract Christians from running the race. One is that strange teachings invariably emphasise the outside observance rather than the inward experience. Sunday observance is yet another weird teaching that has led many Christians into legalism. Jesus emphasised again and again that true purity is not outward but inward. We recall that when they criticised him for not washing his hands before a meal, he said, "It's not what goes into a man's mouth that makes him impure, it's what comes out of his mouth that makes him impure." This is the emphasis of Christ. When we look to Christ, we are not led astray into teaching of outward observances. Rather do we say: I am nourished and strengthened not by eating this food or not eating that food, but in my heart by grace — that is true nourishment.

I can apply it even to Holy Communion. If that becomes an outward observance and you think the bread and the wine is somehow holy food that in itself nourishes you, then read this verse in Hebrews. What nourishes you when you take the bread and wine of Holy Communion is the grace that is at work in your heart. If that is not operating then it does you no good at all and can even do you harm. So the epistle says, "Ceremonial foods are of no value to those who eat them. Our hearts are strengthened by grace." Invariably, false teaching not only emphasises outward observance but minimises the place of grace.

I have examined many false teachings in my time and I am impressed that again and again these weird ideas that get hold of Christians minimise grace and put the emphasis on what we do for God rather than what he does for us. They put the emphasis on the grind rather than the grace of the Christian life, on trying rather than trusting.

So that is the first guideline. If you are going to run the race, don't get carried away with strange doctrines. Remain sound, orthodox, true to Christ. Test everything by him and his teaching and then you will run the race in a straight line.

The second guideline here is that we must be prepared if we are going to run the race to suffer social disgrace or reproach.

The key word in the next few verses is the word "outside". The Jewish argument continues: Jesus was taken outside the camp to be put to death; the body of the sacrifice was burned outside the camp, therefore if we are going to run to Jesus we have got to run out of the city, out of the camp. We must stand with him — outside what? To the Jewish readers of this letter the writer is saying, You've got to stand outside your former religion. You've got to make a clean break with your background, and you've got to come to Jesus outside that background. When Jesus was pushed outside a city wall to that hill on which he was to die, Judaism was making a final break with him. They were saying, "Out with him, out of our city! He doesn't mix; he is new wine in old wineskins. We can't cope, out with him! The sad fact is that if you are going to get close to Jesus, you will find yourself outside. If you run the race, you run away from cities and camps.

Let me spell this out in simple terms. When a young girl who became a Christian came to Charles Haddon Spurgeon shortly afterwards, she said, "How much of the world shall I have to give up?" He said, "Now don't you worry your heart about that my dear, the world will give you up." That was a very wise word. If you are going to stand with Jesus you will have to stand outside the city—and you discover that fairly quickly. If you are the only Christian in your family, is it not true that you felt again and again that you have to stand with Christ outside the family? If you are the only Christian in the place where you work, when you stand with Jesus you suddenly get the sense, "I'm standing outside the office, outside the factory floor." You are different; you are a social misfit. You are somehow treated as not quite the same. Let's go to Jesus outside the camp.

For many it involves a clear break, and we are often reluctant to face this. For some it is going to mean a total change of their social scene and they are reluctant to do this. They want to add Christ to all that they are already involved in. But for an increasing number of people, as we get nearer to the end of the last days of human history, if we are going to go to Christ it means going outside the camp. It means being willing to suffer social ostracism. It means being willing to be unpopular, willing to be humiliated, willing to be isolated, willing to be left alone, willing to be regarded as odd. It means that we are going to lose out on many of the things the world has. We may not get promotion because of being a Christian. We may not get into the club we wanted to join because of being a Christian. We may not be acceptable in the set we would like to be part of — but Jesus was thrown out. If we are going to run the race looking to Jesus we must be prepared to be lonely, to be cut off, and to be with him outside these things.

It is a hard word but it is a necessary one. For your comfort, you have not really lost anything permanently. You only lost a little earlier what you were going to lose anyway, because the city that you belong to on earth is going to pass away. It is not an enduring city. The social set you belong to won't last you forever, just a few years; you are going to lose it anyway — you are going to say goodbye to it at some stage.

Therefore, we look for a city which is to come; we have no enduring city here. We don't mind being thrown out of a city we were going to lose anyway. We don't mind being thrown out of relationships that were going to be broken anyway, that were only temporary. The glorious thing is that we are going outside one city and we may enter another that will last forever. We are losing some friends and we may gain some friends whom we can have forever. We are losing friends to have one friend who is closer than a brother. This is the glorious exchange. Who is losing anything? We may be losing them a few years earlier than worldlings lose these things, but we are getting forever a city whose builder and maker is God. Is that loss? Never.

When you feel alone, when you feel a bit ostracised, when you feel that you are being pushed out of things because you are a Christian, just bear in mind that Jesus said those who have pushed you out will one day find themselves outside for good, and you will be inside. So let us go to him outside the camp, and it will mean decisive breaks; it will mean being thrust out.

Think of persecuted Christians, many of whom are thrust out, marked, kept out of certain jobs because they are Christians. Go on running your race! Where would you rather be: in a godless society without Christ, or outside a godless society with Christ? That is the choice.

In this section of the epistle, *the third thing about running the race is that we are prepared to live a sacrificial life*. This follows again from the thought of sacrifice that has been running through these first few verses. In the Jewish religion you had to bring a sacrifice when you came to worship; you had to look around your flock not for a little weak lamb that would not fetch anything at the market anyway, but for the very best lamb in your flock without spot or blemish, the one that you could get the best price for, and you had to offer that. Therefore, when you came to worship you came with a sacrifice, and you offered a sacrifice to God.

When Jesus died, all sacrifices like that were finished. There is now one Lamb of God who made a full, perfect and sufficient sacrifice for the sins of the whole world, and his sacrifice is acceptable to God — but never make the mistake of thinking that the idea of sacrifice is finished and that you don't have to bring sacrifice when you come to God.

There are two sacrifices we shall be called upon to offer to God as we run the race. First: the sacrifice of praise. Now, is it a sacrifice? How much does it cost to praise God? Let us start at a very down to earth level. It means that if we come to church to worship God it should cost us something. I think on the whole today it costs young people something to worship God in the morning and it costs older people something to worship God at night. Strange, isn't it, how things work out? But how much does it cost? Or is our worship something of convenience? Do we fit it in at a convenient time of day when we are not likely to be doing anything else? Do we hope it will be over in a sufficiently convenient time for us to go home and get lunch in the oven? Is our worship a sacrifice of praise or is it simply a matter of convenience?

For the first three hundred years of Christianity, Sunday was a working day and Christians went to work every Sunday morning, so they had to worship at four o' clock in the morning and ten o' clock at night. It cost them something to do so; it was a sacrifice of praise.

But go a little deeper—there is an idea abroad that we should praise God when we *feel* like praising him and when we praise him at other times it is hypocrisy. That is one of those strange teachings that the devil has managed to instil. Listen to what the Word of God says, "Offer him the sacrifice of praise continually." Now that will be a sacrifice; that will cost you something. For there will be times when you don't feel like praising God, times when you are weighed down by burdens, when the last thing you want to do is sing. Then it is going to be a sacrifice of praise, isn't it? It is costly. In a sense, you make yourself praise. Let us offer a sacrifice of praise *continually* —not just when we feel like it, not when things are going well, not just when my heart is bubbling over, but when things are going wrong, when things are going badly, let's offer a sacrifice of praise. Praise God—that's a sacrifice and it is pleasing to him. So the issue is: what does our praise cost us?

The second sacrifice we are called on to make here—we can't sacrifice blood, we can't sacrifice a lamb—Christ has done that, but we can sacrifice as we share with other people what God has given us. To do good and to share, don't forget to do this because it is a sacrifice well pleasing to God. Christians are called upon to sacrifice—to sacrifice praise and to sacrifice in sharing. To give up something for the sake of someone else, to share with someone else the good things that God has given you — at cost. Not just to give away something that you could do without, the kind of "jumble sale" Christian mentality — but to give away something that you liked, something that you wanted, something that you felt you couldn't do without. God is very pleased with a sacrifice like that. After all, the point of a sacrifice is to please God primarily.

The fourth guideline is a vital part of running the race and it is that if we are going to run the race looking to Jesus, part of the course is to submit to our elders, to obey our leaders—those in authority over us.

This will come as strange to those who feel that if you look to Jesus you should look to him alone. Now it does not say, "Looking unto Jesus alone" —that is a mistaken interpretation. If we are going to look to Jesus then it involves obeying those to whom he has delegated his authority. If we are going to run the race we shall need to run under leaders. We shall need to be under the protection of elders; every Christian needs this.

When people say to me, "Show me where church membership is in the New Testament," I will nearly always point them to this, v. 17 and say, "Who do you submit to?" You cannot, in these days and our circumstances, accept that and do it without being a member of a church under elders. All of us need the protection of those who are accountable to God for looking after us. God has delegated his authority and we need this discipline.

We must not exaggerate the "authority" of elders. The King James (Authorised) Version includes words like "obey", "rule" and "submit" but none of them occur in the original Greek text and owe more to feudal English society. The Greek words are somewhat softer and may be paraphrased "be open to be persuaded by your leaders and be ready to give way to them." In simple terms: let the leaders lead – and let the followers follow. It is an echo of Deborah's grateful praise (Judges 5:2).

Elders have to be aware that they are to give account to God. That is a solemn and almost horrible thought to one who has been placed in the position of an elder — to realise that one day we shall have to stand before the great Shepherd of the sheep and answer for every counsel we have given to any one of his sheep, and that he will hold us responsible for what we have told them to do. The elder must not be doing it for power or prestige, he has been thrust into it and he is only doing it because he himself is under authority. The sheep is under the under-shepherd's authority because the under-shepherd is under the great Shepherd's authority. An elder must be doing it because he has been told to do it. He knows that he must render his account for his care of the flock. The Greek here is "keeps watch over your soul", and literally: "who loses sleep over your soul". A true elder does suffer from insomnia. A true elder loses sleep over people and is concerned — "Am I giving them the right advice? Am I watching over them as I should? Am I caring for them?" But the motive of the sheep towards the under-shepherd, the elder, should be to make his task as happy a one as possible.

What makes a true elder sad? When a sheep takes no notice of the leadership and gets into trouble and goes astray. It makes one very unhappy. What is the greatest joy you can give your elder? It is the joy that John the Apostle writes in his third letter, "I have no greater joy," he says, "than to hear that my children walk in the truth." You can make your elders happy or sad, and as the writer points out, if you make them sad that is no advantage to you. But if you make them happy, they can look after you all the better.

So the elder's motive in giving leadership needs to be

that he is accountable to God. The Christian's motive in submitting to the elder is to make him happy that his job may not be a burden but a delight and that he may be able to look at the sheep and say, "Look at Mr. So and So. Look at Mrs. So and So. Look at them; they're walking in the truth. They're going further; they're developing; they're going on; they're better Christians now than they were a year ago. They're moving forward." Oh, what a joy it is!

What an anxiety it is when one has to look at a sheep straying or losing the love they had. We usedto pray as elders before services at the church where I ministered, and I think you would have been amazed at how often this prayer is prayed, sometimes about those who will not be in the service because their love is growing cold, because they are not as keen as they were. Time and again that comes up in an elders' prayer meeting because it causes a burden, it causes grief.

Things which have happened in the modern church in the twentieth century serve to point out a need for biblical balance in this None of this means that elders are infallible; they are not popes. They are not to be "heavy" or dictatorial. I have written elsewhere of the importance of believers studying and knowing the scriptures for themselves, and there are responsibilities here for fellowships and for members. Nothing I have said here removes that duty which each Christian and the church has been given. Earlier in this book, I referred to the participation by the members in the church's meetings. The Bible does not license improper exercise of power and authority in Christian fellowships, which sadly is sometimes seen. Moreover, the New Testament has much to teach us about the qualities and behaviour required of leaders and the criteria for their fitness for office, selection, appointment.

Let us return to the matter of the heart of an elder. Robert

Murray McCheyne, that great Scottish pastor, wrote in his diary, "As I was walking in the fields today the thought came over me with almost overwhelming power, that every one of my flock would soon be in heaven or in hell. Oh, how I wished I had a tongue like thunder that I might make all hear, or that I had a frame like iron that I might visit everyone and say, 'Escape for thy life. Ah sinner, you little know how I fear that God would lay the blame for your damnation at my door.'" There is a true elder speaking who is not trying to lord it over someone else, not trying to gain power or prestige, an elder who knows that God has made him responsible for those who run, and who is unhappy when the run becomes a walk, and the walk becomes a standstill, and the standstill becomes a backsliding.

The fifth point is that in running the race we must remember to pray for those who are on Christian service elsewhere.

"Pray for us," says the writer to the Hebrews. Pray for two things: for those within the fellowship who are now serving God elsewhere. Pray first that they may live a consistent life where they are, and that the devil who wants to slander them and accuse them will not have any opportunity to do so. Pray, secondly, that they may be restored to you to have fellowship again. When you pray for the missionaries, pray for those two things primarily: that they may live the life that will commend the gospel, and that they may be restored to us; that we may hear how the Lord has dealt with them and what he has done. It is part of running the race that we pray for those who run the race elsewhere, and that we remember those from the fellowship who now serve him in other fields.

I have got some rather strong ideas on missionary furlough. What has so often happened is that a missionary comes home from the field and instead of being integrated back into the fellowship that has sent them out, and coming right into the fold again, and having fellowship in sharing, they are sent all around the country on deputation raising money at little meeting after little meeting. It is wrong. Let us pray that this pattern may go and that in its place we may see missionaries come back as Paul and Barnabas came back to Antioch to spend a long time in that church sharing what the Lord was doing, working within that church, integrating again. Let us change the pattern of missionary life in this country and give more opportunity — that they may be restored to us and then restored in themselves by so doing.

Finally, vv. 20–21. We have reached the blessing and a magnificent statement. "May the God of peace, who through the blood of the eternal covenant brought back from the dead our Lord Jesus, the great Shepherd of the sheep, equip you with everything good to do his will, and may he work in you what is pleasing to him through Jesus Christ, to whom be glory forever and ever. Amen." That is quite a sentence, isn't it?

In terms of guidelines for running the race: it has got to be God working in you rather than you working for him. If you are going to run the race you will not do it by trying to do things for God, you will do it by letting him do things in you.

It is a profound lesson but it is extraordinary how many Christians have fallen into the trap of thinking that they *trust* for their salvation and then they *try* for their sanctification. They let God forgive them, and then it is up to them to do for God what he wants — but that is not the way. It is all trusting from beginning to end, never trying. We can see that these verses are about the work that God has done for us and in us and it is still his work, that is the secret of it.

When a young couple came to Watchman Nee and said, "Will you please pray that we may be more patient with our children?" He said, "No, I won't." They said, "But it's a disgrace. Here we are a professing Christian home and we're constantly losing our temper with our children, becoming irritated by them and impatient with them. Please pray that we may be more patient." He said, "No, I won't pray that." They said, "Why not?" He said, "Because you'll never succeed in being more patient with your children." "But we want to try. We really want to try." "But you never will." Then Watchman Nee told them the secret. He said, "I will pray that Jesus will come and be patient with your children through you." You see the difference? Instead of trying to be patient, let him work it in us.

What has God the Father done for us? He sent the great Shepherd of the sheep to shed his blood to establish an eternal covenant. He has raised him from the dead. God has done all that for us, but having done all that *for* us he now wants to do so much *in* us. What does he want to do in us? He wants to equip us with everything good to do his will. He not only wants to give us the equipment to do it, he wants to do it with the equipment that *he* may work in us everything that is pleasing to him. You see, the main aim of God sending Christ to die, the main aim of the blood of the eternal covenant, the main aim of the resurrection, what's it all for? It is that you may do his will and please God. *You will never do that unless you let him do it in you.*

The world thinks that being a Christian is trying to do good things for God or your neighbour—they usually forget the first and concentrate on the second. But this is the main idea that the world has of what a Christian is: someone who is trying to do good. It is nothing of the kind—it is someone who is letting God do good in him or her. The world may do many good things but the important thing is not to do good things but to do his will. What we think is a good thing to do may not be his will for us.

The vital thing is to know his will, to do it, to be equipped

227

with all that we need to do it. The glorious thing is that God never calls without equipping. He does not ask you to do anything that he can't do in you. If he calls you to do something and you say, "Lord, I can't do that," he says, "I know you can't. I didn't call you to do it in your own strength. I am going to do it through you." Jeremiah said, "But I'm only a teenager, they'll never listen to me." "But I am with you. I'm going to speak through you."

This is the secret of doing good. Not to try and do good for God, but to let God do good through you. To let him work *in*. "To let him make you perfect," it says. I wish I could translate that word for you. It carries different meanings, that Greek verb, "to make you perfect". It means, "to mend what is broken"; it means, "to make up what is lacking"; it means, "to bring into harmony what is out of harmony", and it means all these things together. That God can amend what is wrong in your life; that God can make up what is lacking, that God can bring into harmony what is discord —isn't that marvellous? That God wants to do this and so he sent his Son to die, to shed his blood. The great Shepherd of the sheep, he raised him from the dead.

This God of power is also the God of peace. The God of peace who did this, the God of power who did this, wants to work in you — and that is the secret of being a good person. Lord, I'm not going to try anymore to be a Christian, just you make me one. I'm not going to try and be patient, just you be patient in me. I'm not going to try and be loving, just shed abroad your love in my heart through the Holy Spirit. Do you see the secret? Suddenly you have hit on the way of doing his will and pleasing him. The people who please God most are not those who do most for him, but those who let him do most in them.

That is what running the race means. In the last analysis it is letting him run in me, letting him keep my legs moving.

It is letting him keep my eyes fixed on Jesus. It is letting him open my home to strangers. It is letting him fill me with love for my fellow Christians. It is letting him keep my marriage right. It is letting him keep my contentment right with my money. It is letting him help me to remember the saints who taught me in the first place. It is being prepared to let him take me outside the camp and suffer reproach. It is letting him make the sacrifice of praise in my heart. It is just letting him. Let go; let God take control; let his Holy Spirit control you.

So we have finished the guidelines for the race. With v. 22 we get to the true postscript of the letter—the personal comments. We now are in the addendum. The letter finished properly with the word "Amen." Why did God want the rest of it in his Word? It is just personal—a bit of news, greetings. Sending greetings is important. The last four verses of Hebrews 13 are saying: Brothers, be open, be receptive. Says the author, he has written you a short letter. I don't know if you consider this a short letter. It can be read in one hour flat and it was meant to be read as a whole in the church to which it was written. It is a brief letter, but he says: let it in; be receptive.

He also says, "Our brother Timothy has been in prison but he's out now and he'll come to you, and I'll come with him. Be receptive to us." It is all, "Be receptive." Be receptive to the Word of God; let it in. Be receptive to the visitors among you. Greet all your leaders and all God's people.

I believe it to be fundamental: it is as important that you stay behind after a service to greet people as it is to worship God in the service. It is part of the Word of God. Have you ever noticed how often at the end of a letter it says "Greet one another"? Greet, greet, greet—that is part of your sacrifice of praise. It is part of your duty to the Lord; it is part of running the race. The people who stay behind are not just those who choose to be sociable and like the option of extra, but they are those who realise that greetings are a part of grace, and to greet one another is part of responding to the Word of God.

Greetings are part of the total running the race, and therefore: those from Italy send you greetings. Those who receive God's Word, even a brief letter like the letter to the Hebrews, those who are receptive and bear with God's Word, those who are receptive to visitors from elsewhere. "Grace upon you all" – grace, for greetings and grace belong to each other.

It has been a holy privilege to take you through the letter to the Hebrews. We have been on mountain tops, we have had visions of the Lord; we have seen him as our High Priest—as better than angels, better than prophets, better than anyone else. We have lifted our eyes right up with all the witnesses of the faith including Abraham and Noah. We have looked at Jesus, and we are looking to be made perfect, complete, in harmony in Christ with all those saints of old. Now we have come down to earth, and in fact, if you have really received the letter to the Hebrews you will greet as many people as you can after a church meeting. It is all of a piece and God is as interested in our greeting one another as the grace he poured out in Jesus Christ.

CONCLUSIONS:
1. Possible to lose salvation
2. Once lost, impossible to recover
3. Predestination requires continued co-operation
4. Holiness is as necessary as forgiveness
5. God is a holy God

VALUE:
1. Bible study
2. Christ-centred
3. Faith-building
4. Backsliding
5. Church membership

Unlocking the Bible
is also available in DVD format from
www.davidpawson.com

Lightning Source UK Ltd.
Milton Keynes UK
UKHW020839190520
363484UK00017B/4788